CONSCIOUSNESS
Where Science & Spirituality Meet

NOV 2 0 2015

 D. R. Toi
223 Southlake Pl.
Newport News, VA 23602-8323

Nov. 22-2015 TO
Dec. 12-2020

Swami Amar Jyoti was one of the most insightful, gentle and inspiring teachers that I was fortunate to meet. His book *Consciousness: Where Science and Spirituality Meet* is one of the best explanations available of the secrets of universal awareness. It makes easily accessible to the modern reader the profound system of Vedanta and its transformative path of Self-knowledge. The book will be of great help to Yoga practitioners, meditators and spiritual aspirants everywhere. We look forward to additional titles in the series of Swamiji's books.

—Dr. David Frawley, D. Litt., author of *Shiva: The Lord of Yoga* and *Ayurvedic Healing: A Comprehensive Guide*

With radiant clarity and vast heart, Swami Amar Jyoti translates thousands of years of Vedanta into vibrant and accessible teachings for all who walk a path of awakening: We are that which we seek, he reminds us. Turn within, and rejoice in the encounter.

—Mirabai Starr, Author of *God of Love: A Guide to the Heart of Judaism, Christianity & Islam*

Americans have been blessed by the presence of many emissaries of India's spiritual treasures. Some are well known; others worked quietly with followers. Swami Amar Jyoti is one of the latter, which makes the publication of this collection a most welcome event. It is an important addition to the ongoing transmission of Vedic wisdom to this part of the globe."

 —Philip Goldberg, author of *American Veda: From Emerson and the Beatles to Yoga and Meditation, How Indian Spirituality Changed the West*

In this beautiful book the ancient wisdom of yoga is retold in the language of today, bringing together Science, Spirituality and Consciousness. Here are stepping stones to take us out of the limited world of ego consciousness into the light of our divine consciousness, and the joy and ecstasy that belong to this light. Swami Amar Jyoti shows us how to be in tune with the real rhythm of creation, with the dance of oneness and the light that is within and all around us. Attuned with what is real, we are no longer imprisoned in illusion. We can realize what we are—that *It is all Light.*

 —Llewellyn Vaughan-Lee, Ph.D., Sufi teacher and author

For readers in search of enlightening, healing words, here is an invitation for a journey into our consciousness. Swami Amar Jyoti articulates the ancient Indian wisdom and its didactic symbols in today's language. This remarkable volume brings the teachings of the East, especially Vedanta, into our age and life. Another beautiful feature of the book is the vast openness in which the concepts are discussed; the reader feels a spirit of peace and compassion on the pages.

—Rasoul Sorkhabi, Ph.D., Professor of Geology, writer and poet

The words he offers are like echoes of a hugeness, a vastness... He is you and me together as One. To have access to a *Wisdom Library* of his work, right at your fingertips, is a rare gift. For that, all of us can be grateful.

—P. M. H. Atwater, L.H.D. near-death researcher and author, including *Dying to Know You: Proof of God in the Near-Death Experience, and Children of the Fifth World*

CONSCIOUSNESS
Where Science & Spirituality Meet

WISDOM LIBRARY OF SWAMI AMAR JYOTI
VOLUME 1

TRUTH CONSCIOUSNESS
Desert Ashram, Tucson, Arizona USA

By Swami Amar Jyoti

SPIRIT OF HIMALAYA
The Story of a Truth Seeker

RETREAT INTO ETERNITY
An Upanishad—Book of Aphorisms

IN LIGHT OF WISDOM
Spontaneous Poetry for the Soul

ESPÍRITU DE HIMALAYA
La Historia de un Aspirante de la Verdad (Spanish)

THE LIGHT THAT AWAKENS
A Guidebook to Higher Consciousness

About Swami Amar Jyoti

IMMORTAL LIGHT
The Blissful Life and Wisdom of Swami Amar Jyoti
Edited and Compiled by Sita Stuhlmiller

For more information
SwamiAmarJyoti-Books.org

When your mind is still, the Light shines.
Then you will see the whole cosmic dance—
how it moves, creates and dissolves;
how every split second it changes patterns,
colors and sounds. At that moment you are freedom
and bliss—Satchidananda.

SWAMI AMAR JYOTI

CONTENTS

Preface   *xi*

Introduction   *xiii*

1   Unlocking the Mysteries of Creation   *1*

2   What is Illusion? What is Reality?   *17*

3   The Dance of Creation   *33*

4   The Illusion of Space, Time and Ego   *49*

5   Unveiling the Secrets of the Universe   *67*

6   Illusion, Reality and the New Age   *81*

7   Lord Shiva's Dance   *93*

8   Beyond Time and Space   *101*

Poem: In Radiant Expanse of Limitless Space   *119*

Notes   *121*

Bibliography   *123*

About the Author   *125*

Truth Consciousness and Ashrams   *129*
founded by Swami Amar Jyoti

PREFACE

Recordings of the *Satsangs* of Swami Amar Jyoti were
first made available on audiocassette to a small group of
devotees in 1974. Until His Mahasamadhi in 2001, each
of his Satsangs was recorded live. Over seven hundred
recordings are still available on CD and MP3 downloads.
Edited versions of these profound and deeply inspiring
teachings also have been published for decades in *Light
of Consciousness—Journal of Spiritual Awakening.*
In response to repeated requests that the Satsangs
be presented in book form, it is a privilege to launch
the *Wisdom Library of Swami Amar Jyoti, beginning
with Volume 1: Consciousness: Where Science and
Spirituality Meet.*

Gurudeva often spoke of how one day spirituality
and science would merge, as scientists and spiritual
seekers meet in their quest for what the scientists
sometimes call the Unified Field—synonymous with
Consciousness, God, Brahman, the Absolute, Eternal,
Light, the Divine. Through these Satsangs this ancient
wisdom is approachable not only for the scholarly or
the adept but for all who come with an open mind and
heart. As Gurudeva reveals:

When you will, one-hundred-percent, to know the secret of your own life, you shall arrive at the highest discovery: the Light, the Divine within you. The sages, Enlightened Beings and Prophets are telling us that this is possible for everyone. They show the way because potentially everyone is Divine; everyone is Light. We are made of that Consciousness.

The Master is known for the simplicity and clarity with which He imparts the infinite wonders and luminous glory of the cosmos, Creator and Creatrix. May you find inspiration and enlightenment in this sublime wisdom.

Sita Stuhlmiller

Marianne Martin

INTRODUCTION

OM ASATO MA SADGAMAYA
TAMASO MA JYOTIRGAMAYA
MRITYOR MA AMRITAMGAMAYA
OM SHANTI SHANTI SHANTI

.

Lead us from the unreal to the eternal truth,
from darkness to light,
from death to the nectar of immortality.
May there be peace, peace, peace.

—Brihadaranyaka Upanishad

ACCORDING TO THE YOGA TRADITION, an
Enlightened sage is one who has transcended the
instinctive tendency of identifying himself (or herself)
as an isolated, bodily individual in an external, largely
uncaring world. The sage experiences an infinite,
eternal and divine consciousness. Confusion of identity
ceases and the purpose of life is revealed. He knows
himself to be the ocean of existence, of which all life
is but an expression of his own delight and creativity.
I believe that Swami Amar Jyoti is such a sage.

An authentic Guru is one who is Enlightened and, simply as a result of compassion, spends his life attempting to share with others the consciousness he enjoys. This demands a love and commitment to service that is almost impossible to conceive. He spends his life loving others more than they love him. I believe Swami Amar Jyoti is such a Guru.

The reader who is familiar with the life of Swami Amar Jyoti (henceforth referred to as Gurudeva, "Divine Teacher") may find my referencing him in the present tense unusual in light of his Mahasamadhi in 2001. Allow me to explain. I became aware of Gurudeva and his teachings shortly after his passing when I became a reader, and later a contributor, to *Light of Consciousness,* a magazine published by his disciples. I noticed a striking and inexorable occurrence with the publication of each issue: in every new copy, a transcribed talk or Satsang by Gurudeva remarkably, precisely, and unmistakably addressed my life and what I was contemplating at that time. When such an event happens once, it is a coincidence. When it happens every time, there is something more profound at work.

As I read Gurudeva's works over the years, my personal experience increasingly became that I was not so much reading the recorded statements of a sage no longer with us. I felt as if I was receiving a series of letters from someone who was dropping timely notes in my mailbox about current events. Gurudeva was not far away at all; he was just about as near as I would allow him to be.

This recognition of Gurudeva being alive with us, regardless of the status of his physical form, reached a culmination for me during a private retreat in May of 2015. At that time, it became clearly obvious to me that a physical body is irrelevant for a sage of Swamiji's caliber. From this perspective, this book is not a record or historical document; it is a living and vital transmission of an ever-timely wisdom and love.

Children are naturally curious and adventurous. As we grow older we usually replace exploration with the pursuit of security and comfort. Yet those who are not satisfied with the mundane world search for a path and a guide. Gurudeva Swami Amar Jyoti is a rare being, a true and capable guide. This book is a map by which to navigate the mundane world of contraction and fear, and enter into the divine world of love and light. Gurudeva is at times strict and uncompromising, remonstrating that we need not settle for superficial lives of little importance. Other times, he is like a sweet and doting Mother, cajoling reluctant little ones to accept the precious gifts being offered.

Some of the teachings in this book may challenge your closely held beliefs. Good. In order to come into the Kingdom of God, we need to leave our old world behind. This is not done by dying; it is accomplished by awakening into eternal life. We need to be willing to challenge the paradigm we have constructed that describes who we are and how the world operates. We need, in essence, the humility to be wrong and the courage to change.

The authority in Gurudeva's words provides the aspirant with the comfort that it is safe to release our mental and emotional security blankets. Gurudeva, like all authentic spiritual guides, issues no dictatorial ultimatums. Quite the contrary: he provides support for intuition, assurance of capability, and inspiration for accomplishment.

If a wealthy man came to your town and offered you riches beyond belief, most likely you would heartily accept his gift. I sincerely believe there is nothing in the rich man's wallet that approaches the fortune to be found in this book. Gurudeva has opened the divine vault and welcomes us into a treasure trove. This is the wine of the yoga sages poured into a new bottle that we of the modern day can imbibe and appreciate. I encourage you to accept this book as a gift of wisdom, of love, and blessings that are capable of transforming life into a dance of eternal light, joy and peace.

Prem Prakash
Green Mountain School of Yoga
Middlebury, Vermont

UNLOCKING THE MYSTERIES OF CREATION

You mentioned that this is all a dream. Who does the dreaming?

THE SIMPLEST REPLY IS, the dreamer dreams. However, to elaborate, let us begin with the example of dreaming in normal life. Everyone dreams in sleep. However, the three states of sleep—deep dreamless sleep, dreaming during sleep, and what we call being awake, are really all *within* the dream. How this happens perhaps would answer your question.

The first Creator, let us say God—whether the Biblical conception of God or the Vedic *Brahman*[1]—created. According to Vedic belief, God has three aspects: Creator, Preserver, and Destroyer or Transformer. When He creates we call Him Brahma; when He maintains we call Him Vishnu; when He destroys or transforms we call Him Shiva. According to the Bible also, God created everything. God originally created you and me, Adam and Eve.

According to the *Vedas*, Brahma first created ego, which is the sense of "I"-ness with nothing beyond it. Simply "I," not "I am." This level of I-ness can be compared to deep, dreamless sleep. There you and I exist, with nothing beyond it. In deep sleep we are not even aware of being "I" until we come to another level

of consciousness such as dreaming or waking. Then
we say we slept very nicely, we did not even dream, or
at least we do not recall dreaming. When you awaken
from such sound sleep, you feel refreshed.

I (EGO)   This sense of I-ness, which we call ego, is the first
creation of God or Brahma. This "I" has a will—not

Will   Supreme Will but limited will—percolating from the
Will of God. As God willed, ego then wills. But when
ego wills, we call it desire. God wills—man desires.

Desire =   This desire is the first vibration we create from the
our First   unit called "I." As if ego is a center, a kind of dot, then
Vibe
it becomes a line. It expands and creates a wave, a
vibration. This is the basis of consciousness.

Conc.   In the waveless ocean of Consciousness, the
ego wills or desires. This produces motion and is the

dream   beginning of the *dream*. The total picture of any dream,
whether complex or simple, vivid or indistinct, is due to
many vibrations—wills and desires—being released by
the ego simultaneously. During sleep, these vibrations
become so jumbled up with each other that they produce

Sleep =   meaningless dreams, as you know. However, even those
meaningless dreams are a filtration of the mind. When

Mind   your dreams become very vivid, easily understandable,
and seem to be related to the future, past or present,

Lucid   then you are quite concentrated and distinct about
willing and desiring. Otherwise your jumble of desires

creates dreams that are like abstract art: a hodgepodge
of uncontrolled and unguided desires. Such dreams have
their value, however. If they would not be there, life
would be a greater burden. Much is released in dreams.

Will or desire sets the ocean of consciousness into
motion, producing waves, seemingly formulations.
Then the dream, which actualizes on the astral plane,
becomes a physical materialization. It becomes grosser,
more thickened and sensual, meaning: perceivable by
the senses. But the dreamer who dreams is you and me,
that unit called I-ness, the first creation. However, there
are many mansions in my Father's house—we are not
talking of only two rooms, but rooms within rooms:
me, my dreams and my physical world. Beyond this
there is a stage of true awakening where all this is seen
as a dream. But throughout all these mansions, *me* is
a common factor.

The sense of I-ness, the ego or root, holds all these
worlds together. *I* is controlling all your worlds, the
dreamlands as well as the physical lands. Where *you*
finish, your dreams finish. You may ask why dreams
continue if we do not want them. Simply out of habit
or karma already recorded. The recording has become
so embedded in the fabric of our minds that the dreams
just go on playing. We are not able to stop them because
they are not consciously guided or directed by us. If

we could direct and control our dreams, they could
be channeled or stopped, as with any other kind of
recording when we know how to use the equipment.

If you cultivate this direction and control, it brings
you back to the dreamer, to that awareness: "I am
dreaming." There is a beautiful point in this: not only
are these dreams, created by waves in the ocean of
consciousness, seemingly outside you, but the scriptures
have gone so far as to say, "You are dreaming within
you." *Within you* does not refer only to your body, it
means that ego unit. Within this one microscopic unit of
I or ego—one dot or atom only—you have the universe
inside you. It is very difficult to visualize this point, but
if you concentrate it can be very clearly understood.
That is why the famous Vedantic aphorism: *You
perceive only what you are*, which means: *everything
is within you*. Not only within you, inside your heart or
soul, but the whole phenomenon is taking shape within
that *you* or *I* unit, that nucleus. The formulation is
within you, like the waves on the ocean.

To visualize this by intellect alone is difficult. It
can verily be realized when you emerge from *samadhi*.[2]
We say then that you are superconscious. When you
come back to your True Self, all this becomes clearly
apparent. It is as if you enter the gate or door to
Yourself. There you will find that this manifestation,

this radiation out of you, is not outside you. It is within you. Let us take for example the sun in the sky: the sun's rays are projected to all the planets. As far as the rays reach, you could call that the sun's radiation. Can we say where the sun ends and the sunshine begins? Even so, the Self is not this one unit only but wherever *Self* your radiation goes. Where your manifestation or the creation is, there is your Self. So, everything is within the Self.

When you enter that tiny door of your Self, when you truly go within, you will find that God is within *God* you. It is as if that dot—symbolized in the OM (symbol) as a dot on the top of the crescent—opens. That dot is the supreme transcendence. You are entering into your Self. The dreams and visualizations are just you. In other words, the dream and the dreamer are not two. *dreamer = one* Subject, object and relationship—the trinity—join into one. Everything is within you. You are everything. I am everything. It is all within me.

To take another example, we are sitting in this hall. Seemingly I am here, you are there, and we are talking. We are aware of many things. Because of our present level of consciousness, we see distances, time and space, things separate from each other. But if you are in *samadhi* that superconscious state of samadhi, whether your eyes are open or not, all you will see is within you! You will

not see a room full of separate people. You will see
the panorama within your body or mind, however you
name it. Within your *being* you will see all this. This
realization is the highest pinnacle, the climax of *Vedanta.*[3]
The question may arise, if this is all within me, then what
about others? Are they also seeing everything within
them? How can all this be in so many persons? This is
a very sound question, but it does not remain when you
see that *all is you.*

Language cannot reach us to the perfect realization
of such things. You have to go into superconsciousness
to see this. In that trance, that reverie or deep meditation,
you will see within you *everything*. To any end of
eternity, of infinity, wherever your conception or
consciousness projects, you will see it is *you*. You will
no longer be this individual body. You or I will extend
infinitely and eternally. Within your projection this
phenomenon *exists*. Thus the famous saying, *God
created out of Himself.*

Now if God created out of Himself, where did
He keep it? Outside Him? He created *out* of Himself
within Himself. We say "out of" for explanation's
sake. There is no within and without in God—God is
everywhere. Where is within and without then? But
just for play's sake we say within and without, inside

and outside. Again, this can only be realized after reaching the superconscious state, not before. Wherever your ideas, thoughts or mind extend, it is *you*. Within the atom the whole universe plays. And when you go deep within you will find that there is only One in the whole universe, no one else. When you achieve that transcendence, it is only *You*.

ONE is
You

Not only is it out of you, as in multiplication, but it is all within you. If you break a stone into many pieces, it is the same stone. If it were to break into millions and billions of particles, still it would be from that original stone. The whole universe is like that, dualism versus non-dualism, relativity versus Absolute. But these are not two. Relativity plays within the Absolute; dualism plays within non-dualism. One saint explained this in his simple rural colloquialism: "I keep non-dualism in my pocket and play with dualism."

Such concepts cannot be understood philosophically; they have to be taken in and meditated upon deeply. Then you will see. This is the basis of the *Maha Vakyas* or great Vedic aphorisms: *I Am That, Thou art That.* This is not only liberation or salvation; it is beyond words and thoughts, where dreams end. When you reach this realization, you will see that we are visualizing and seeing a creation of our own desires, nothing else.

dreamer = me

And "me" is the dreamer of those dreams, the creator
of that creation. Not only so but me is that creation.
The world is God. Sometimes people misconstrue this,
saying, "Since God is within the world also, why not
be worldly?" This is a corruption of that realization.
Without attaining superconsciousness we cannot say
the world is God. After all, how many see the world
as God, as Me, or as Oneness?

God   Not only did God create the world, He made the
world out of Him. And if He created out of Him, it must
be *He.* Let's put our concentration on this. If God made
the world out of Him, what will it be? God again. A
pot made out of clay is clay. A pot made out of silver
is silver. The universe made out of God *is* God. What
makes it different from God? Dualism. Before it was
only silver; now it is a silver pot. But the silver and pot
are not two things. It is still as much silver as it was
before being made into a vessel. What is the difference?
It has been given form. Previously it was a lump of
silver without shape. Once it has form, we give it a
name. We call it a pot. This is called dualism—form and
name. That is why it is called a dream, because the pot
is not eternally existent, comparatively, as silver is. The
form is a conception and the conception is a name called
pot. Break the pot into pieces; it is gone. The dream is
over. What remains? Silver. Even though broken into

pieces and no longer a pot, you still call it silver. This is called birth and death: birth of a pot, death of a pot. In both conditions the silver remains silver throughout. In creation, God remains God throughout. You can replace this concept with another term: Consciousness, Light, Awareness, whatever you call it.

Throughout it is so. The emanation of God must be God, whether the form changes or not. In all the three conditions—creation, preservation, destruction— deep sleep, the dream state and waking—*you* remain. It is your dream, your physical world, you in deep sleep. Throughout you are *you.* Only conceptions change, forms change, names change. We call this birth and death. The entire creation, preservation and transformation incessantly carries on *through* you, *by* you, *in* you. And we go on creating and seeing this whole dream all the time, including its refreshments and fatigues. All is within the dream—young age, old age, death and birth. The Trinity—creation, preservation, destruction—are within that formation and annihilation.

Another example is water. Its formations of steam, liquid and ice are all within the same substance. Vapor, clouds, rain and rivers are all within the same substance, the same drama. And the dream *is* a drama. Using the example of the pot again: within the pot there is air or space and outside the pot there is also air or space. One side of the pot we call outside, the other side we call inside. But inside and outside it is the same space. If you break the pot, the inside and outside mingle, but even before that, it was the same space inside and out. What differentiated or separated it was the wall of the pot. The wall or shape is called form, dualism. Again, put sea water in the pot and set it to float upon the ocean. The water is the same inside and outside the pot, we simply call it inside and out. But if you break the pot, the inner water mingles with the ocean. It becomes one. What was the wall in between? What was the point of separation? The form. We are all "pots."

This is the whole mystery of the phenomena of creation that scientists are researching: the secret to creation is dualism, created form and name, which today is called relativity. If you want to understand the universe, not only this earth but to any infinity or eternity, understand these two components, form and name. You will understand everything. There is no creation outside of dualism. Try to conceive anything without form or name; you will not be able to do so. To give shape and name *is* creation. And because the form is transitory, conceptual and limited—not eternal—we call it a dream. A dream is that which is impermanent. Absolute reality is not a dream because it does not change.

When we say to be detached from this world, this dream, we are just telling you to be detached from the unreal. You are dreaming and your pain and miseries are within the dream. Why not go to the root cause of the problem? The root cause of miseries is our insatiable running after fleeting mirages of changeful phenomena. Looking to the transitory for satisfaction is what creates misery.

What we call creation is changing phenomena. That is why Realized Souls say to be detached from form and name and be attached, or rather devoted, to the contents. Do not look to the pot, look to the contents. Identify yourself with the form and name— you will have to lament. Identify yourself with the Reality—you will not lament. Happiness is the breeding ground for unhappiness. At no stage should we be attached to and identified with the changing phenomena. If we do, we are foolish, ignorant.

Whatever the world is, it is not wrong. The Creator is the foundation of all this, the *Summum Bonum*, the Essence, the Spirit, the Light. Because of that Light *Light* we exist. The question could be asked: what about darkness? How was it created? Darkness was not created; it is not a commodity or manifestation. If you go deep into darkness, you will see light. Anything that you see is because of Light. The answer lies in how you see or perceive the darkness. With what knowledge or sense of existence do you see the darkness? With what light do you see the darkness? With the light of awareness. We are *aware* of darkness. How otherwise could you say it is darkness?

By the same example, unless we are awakened to non-dualism, to the Absolute, we cannot really *know* what dualism is. We are in the dream—action and reaction, cause and effect, form and name—and we philosophize so much that we take it to be real. If it is Real it should not give us pain and misery. It should not give us stagnation or a sense of separation. The Truth should not be painful. That which gives us pain, which makes us miserable, or wanting, must be unreal. This is dualism.

Our folly is not awakening. We want to "sleep" because it is comfortable. But sleep can be comfortable only up to some limits. Beyond that it becomes drudgery, and that is the very drudgery we carry through life. Sleep carried too far is stagnation and suffering. When we awaken, we come back to our Absolute Truth: *I am*. Me as Awareness, me as Absolute, me as God, as Light, as Infinite, Eternal, without name and form. That unlimited Consciousness is blissful.

That which God created out of Himself has been eulogized in the Vedas:

OM Poornamadah Poornamidam
Poornaat Poornaamudachyate
Poornasya Poornamaadaaya
Poornamevaavashishyate

"From Perfection we are born, in Perfection we live, in Perfection we shall end." But how to realize this? We must awaken from our dreams. Awakening is the answer.

·2·

WHAT IS ILLUSION? WHAT IS REALITY?

This morning, I read a quote from a scientist who said that Light is the closest science has come to the *Light* **Absolute. He called Light the bridge between the material and the spiritual.**

TO SAY THAT LIGHT is bridging the material world and the spiritual is to divide them into two things. This is the fundamental fallacy. From the spiritual to *Reality is* the most dense matter, it is one continuity. This is the way conception creates its own reality. In dualism, in relativity, you have myriads of forms and names and each assumes individuality: matter is one individuality, the spiritual world is another, and a bridge is needed between the two. This is the basic fallacy inherent in intellect, which is itself the product of dualism. Intellect cannot go outside its own campus; it wants to explain, analyze and then synthesize.

  If we start from this premise, then the statement that Light is the closest representation to the Absolute also falls flat. Even if we separate the material world and spiritual world conceptually, nothing in creation *(onc.* can exist without some Substance or Consciousness within it. That is, within all conception or illusion there is a degree of Light or Consciousness without which it would not exist. But it is so unmanifest, so concealed— yet so intrinsic—that to see it as Light is difficult. From gross matter to the ultimate Spirit, there is no gap. The difference is only in the degree of manifestation.

Matter's own reality, if you care to find it, will be in atoms, particles, sub-particles. Go to any limit—that will be Light, Consciousness. To our conceptual view, matter looks inert, inanimate or dead. If it were dead, matter would crumble, disintegrate and then transform into something else again. But Light is throughout, continuous. That is why sages have said: "All is Divine." When they say "all," there is no exception; it includes illusions, conceptions, matter—*everything* is Divine. Everything is intrinsically made of Light. It's a matter of finding that out. When you use the faculty of analysis you are bound to make mistakes because you divide and separate and compare, and then try to bridge it all up again. Synthesis is not part of modern science yet. To me it is fully satisfying to say, "It is all God."

Then what is illusion? If it is not Reality, then what is it? Because illusion, *maya*, is somewhat perceptible or conceivable, in a certain limited area of reality, it has its own existence of which you and I are a part. What is the reality of illusion, then? If everything is Divine and everything is Light, then illusion must have the same basis. Whatever the reality of its existence may be, it is *something*. If there is Light within illusion, then illusion assumes some kind of existence.

Shankaracharya[4] explained this very beautifully. He said: "Illusion appears to be real but is not really so." It is an appearance only. It has some kind of formation, a temporary existence, but since it is not absolute or eternal, we cannot call it Reality. Still the question remains, what is illusion? We are part of illusion; that is the problem. Illusory beings are trying to understand illusion! One sage has given a very good reply: "If darkness is trying to understand darkness, it will never know since it is darkness itself. But bring in Light and darkness vanishes. It is simply not there."

The mind cannot know or understand maya, its *Mind* own illusory nature. To do that, it has to surrender or merge into Reality. It has to transcend ego, limited conceptual existence, in order to know the Reality. If all is Divine, then illusion is also Divine. I am stretching the logic but if you want to face the truth, you have to ask bold questions. If everything is Divine—physical, mental, spiritual—and if illusion is Divine, then what is its nature? Let's assume for the time being, in order to understand, that there are three stages, the gross, inert, immovable matter that is *Matter* Light; the vibratory or ethereal, which is more subtle than matter, is also Light; and the non-conceptual, non-dualistic, which is Absolute Light in its own true pristine form. Throughout Light is playing continuously

LIGHT

in various phenomena. That means what? Throughout creation there is a continuity of Light manifested in greater and lesser degrees. Light is always within everything. Since Light is inseparable from nature, the phenomena, and continuous, sages have called it the maintenance or sustenance aspect of creation. And that is maya, the matrix, which we call Divine Mother.

Let's put it this way: if the Light had no phenomena, gross or subtle, if it were devoid of nature or cosmic energy, creation would not exist. To make creation flourish is the work of the Creatrix in the aspect of maintainer and sustainer. She is inseparable from the Divine, from Light, and pervaded throughout creation.

Maya
This is the fact of maya, that although it is changeful, shifting, perceptual and conceptual, at the same time it is fully Divine. It is so interrelated and intermixed with Absolute Truth and Light that it is Divine, as is everything. It is not only respect for matter and illusion that I am talking about, it is accepting God's phenomena as godly. Then there is no question of bridging anything. Bridging is only needed when you forget, when there is a gap in your thought process. Then you bridge it as a kind of intellectual gymnastics. There has to be a coherence of thinking.

Whatever we have been condemning as illusion, whatever we think is worldly, or degrading by

characterizing it as non-divine, we are giving that
thing or action the potency to degrade us. Start
from the premise: all is divine; all is godly. It is
only a matter of relative and Absolute. Even a great
sage such as Shankaracharya rejected the idea that
illusion is un-Divine. He gave the example that if
we say a lotus is blooming in the sky—that is a non-
existent phenomenon. It has no reality because the
lotus does not bloom in the sky. It is a total myth,
unreal. Something that is perceivable to the senses has
existence, but from the eternal point of view, it is illusory *Senses*
because it is not permanent. Therefore Shankaracharya
said that the phenomena, *jaggat,* the cosmos, is "non- *Cosmos*
existent existence." It appears to be real but it is not
truly Real. We call this divine phenomenon Mother
because She maintains the creation. Otherwise, Light
or the Absolute would go from point to point, dazzling
in its own pristine purity, and the creation would be
non-existent. But creation is existent in its own way.
Therefore, we worship this Divinity. This is God and
you also.

Do not ask, "So if everything is Divine, then is evil
Divine?" We can argue these points before Realization
but after Realization these questions do not exist. They
won't even be in your conceptions. So I always feel,
humbly, that if we could correct our premises then

many problems will be over. Why? Due to ages of karmas and *samskars*—impressions, modifications or habits—the mind has the tendency to try to corner the Truth, to question, to be skeptical, because that gives it a little gratification of personality. It creates *reductio ad absurdum* arguments that will eventually prove null and void. But until then the mind gets to survive, which is what it wants. It has a habit of skepticism, and when that proves foundationless, it creates resistance in order to save itself. If resistance doesn't work, it denies. If denial doesn't work, it escapes. If escape doesn't work, then it threatens suicide, but it won't give up. This is just a survival instinct of ego.

But amazingly this mind, which is a mass of illusions, is also Light. It has the capacity to cover up the Light if it chooses. But if you have the will to penetrate through your mind you will be awakened and light-full. Anything, even a stone, if you search for its ultimate particle or substance, is Light. So it is with the mind. When you look at it directly, boldly and deeply, it will reveal its Light. And that is Divine Mother's form. Therefore we love Her, we are devoted to Her, as She is maintaining all this creation.

God the Father and God the Mother are inseparable. Divine Mother is not dependent upon Divine Father but She has no existence of Her own. Together in union,

Purusha and *Prakriti,* create and maintain. The Creator cannot do without the Creatrix and the Creatrix cannot do without the Creator. They are Spirit and Nature, like milk and its whiteness. Whiteness is not dependent upon milk, nor is milk dependent upon whiteness; they are one and the same.

When we analyze or theorize and say, "This is Father, this is Mother, this is energy, this is the substance..." that is only conceptual thinking. For the play's sake, for the phenomena's sake, we do talk of two, but really both are One. This is a matter of Realization, not of intellectual understanding. It is there within everything, every particle. When Light reveals, you see it in everything. Then you will lose the differentiation of enemy and friend, evil and virtue, because they do not exist in that state of being. When you see the Light, there are no sins or crimes. In that Realization the mind transcends its own limits.

Divine Mother is capable of assuming any form. That doesn't mean She cannot exist as a person, as an entity, as a Goddess—She does—but it depends on which form you want to see. She is supreme, infallible, pervading. In other words, the creation is beginningless and endless. Everywhere you go is Divine. If you have opened up your consciousness, everywhere you go is Light. If you are awakened, then Divine Mother is everywhere beautiful. Also, relatively speaking, when you are calling Her Divine Mother, you are assuming you are a child. And if you are Her child, you are supposed to be childlike. Otherwise, if you call Her and keep up your front of ego-personality, She is not Mother for you. You have to be childlike. Jesus said, "Let the little children come to me and do not hinder them, for the kingdom of God belongs to such as these."

Same The Creator and creation are not two; they are inseparable and the same. When you Realize this, you will know the mysteries of creation, how it is all happening. It looks very complex, beyond our comprehension, but actually it is very simple. If you reach that pinnacle of wisdom, mysticism and alchemy become simple for you to understand. That is where you are lord, not over others or Lord of the universe, but lord in your own self as supreme. Nothing is hidden from you. And you achieve this simply by being a child of Divine Mother.

On the relative plane She is benevolent, She is the Protectress, She hears, She helps, She removes obstacles, She nurtures. But in the Absolute sense, Divine Mother becomes part and parcel of your expression and manifestation. That is your ultimate, true, absolute identity. And therefore Divine Mother, illusion, supreme energy and matter are at your fingertips, a part of you, from you, existing in you and you existing in That. The division is lost and that is the full, satisfying Realization. Losing nothing, gaining nothing. You live in perfection, you die in perfection. Everything is fulfilling and satisfying.

It is within that you awaken, that you avoid the clouds of perception and conception, and get to the Absolute, called *Kevalya* in Sanskrit. When you truly awaken it is all Divine; it's all conscious play; it's all your True Being. There was no non-being. So let us not waste energy in mental pursuits that do not mean anything. The easier way is to go directly to Divine Mother. Since we are in the phenomena and phenomenal beings ourselves—our body, mind and vital—we can only start from where we are. And that is the Mother we worship, *Shakti*, Divine Energy.

As we are now, we meditate, we focus on the goal, but still it is illusion. You are imagining something: God or the cross or Om or Light. You are taking shelter under that very illusion which is Divine Mother. And then with the help of this illusion you focus. Gradually you will see that She goes on revealing more and more— beyond what you would have thought or imagined. She knows everything because She is everything. Only you as a child have to merge into That. Just be like a child, simple and innocent, and approach Her. Do not

tell Her you know a few things but now your boat is
stuck, "so please tell me only this much." What if that
point is connected with many other points? You cannot
isolate a point and tell Divine Mother, "Don't touch my
other points!" Even if you understand something, who
is giving a guarantee that you understand rightly? What
if your whole understanding is built upon fallacies? So
when you honestly approach God or Divine Mother,
They are going to open your whole file. That is why
you are afraid to approach. The truth is that God and
Divine Mother already know everything. You are hiding
from you, blinding yourself only. And in order to make
your blindness successful you resist; you get skeptical.
And that is a tragedy.

No part of our mind is isolated enough not to
deal with other aspects of our mind. When you are
approaching one aspect of your mind the Supreme is
bound to open other aspects. They are interrelated. You
cannot say, "God, I just came here to ask You such and
such boon." He will ask you connected questions. And
that is where you hide; you do not want to be touched.
On one side, it is scary to be exposed. But see the
beauty: even that very moment, when Divine Mother is
exposing you or questioning you, She is giving you an
opportunity to clean up and get rid of those things you
are hiding. If She is not forcing you, it is only because

MMD

you do not want it, not because She does not want to help you. Could She not still force you then? Yes, but why should She? It is your problem, not Hers. She will not force you to change. In Her Divine creation, She is perfectly fine. She allows us to be foolish. This is the benevolence of Divine Mother.

We do not see that we are simply actors and someone else is running the whole show. It is all illusion, no doubt about it, but again within this illusion, there is *Light*. If you could awaken and be conscious, all your problems would be over. Divine Mother is really very benevolent. She is *Karuna-mayi,* the Compassionate One. She is *Jyotir-mayi,* full of Light. She is *Tejo-mayi,* Radiant. She is so available to all, if we can just be Her children. And the greatest part is that in no time, with this attitude of a child, She erases all our dross, sins, infirmities and incapacities. If I had not experienced this, I would not speak in this way. She will erase lifetimes and lifetimes of sins, weaknesses and infirmities, when we come to Her with simplicity, innocence and selfless devotion. Even if She would chastise, it is in such a sweet manner that you will know She is your Mother, and your illusions will drop off.

It is amazing that Mother Divine could be synonymous with illusion, but again, She is so real. The Light within illusion will shine in such a way that you will not see a difference between the Light and no light. It is all Light, all Divine. Through that phenomenon you get Absolute Realization. If you approach with devotion, selflessness and childlike simplicity, She reveals Herself in no time. It is not only a rare prayer that will make Her hear you; it needs regular contact, establishing a relationship with Her as a true Mother. Any problem—material, relationships, spiritual, health— if you latch on to Her, somehow hold on to Her Feet, you will see Her mercy.

Do not take Divine Mother as simply an entity by Herself. She is One with the Absolute, the Spirit, Light. Keep your mind on That. And it is very simple in the sense that in many other Yoga practices you have to do much hard work, but in this approach, as a child, you do not have to do anything. Just give up unto Her and She does everything for you. If you are truly honest and sincere, She really listens. See in this way; be conscious. Then you are not only a channel of God, you are God's own. You find Oneness in everything. There you and I are not different. Not only "God working through me"—we *are* He, *Aham Brahman Asmi*.[5] And there you transcend all time and space conceptions.

We are living in the *Kali Yuga*, the Iron Age, a very materialistic age, and if you cannot do austere, complex yogic feats, you can do simple things. Approach God or Divine Mother as a child. Even in this Kali Yuga, everything is Light. You can be awakened. You can raise your consciousness. Pray to Divine Mother to help you, to protect you, to purify you. She does it in no time. And She gives you indications and glimpses: "It is done, don't worry." Whatever astrology or psychology may say, She can transcend all these calculations and do the impossible. Just be an innocent child. Be joyful. Find oneness with all. Still you can act and live as a human, social being, very perfectly. Hide nothing. Sit in meditation with a pure heart and pray to God, "Let me be awakened. Make me conscious that Thou art not only in me but we are the same. To that stage of godliness, please raise me." Ask for more than your daily bread. Pray, "Let my life be fulfilled. Let me come out of this unconsciousness and ignorance." God and Divine Mother listen. Your potential is more than you know. You are given great opportunities all the time to come out of ignorance. Make use of these opportunities. With a pure heart, like a child, pray, "Lord, let me be awake as Thou art. Let me be One with You." It is not an abstract idea. It works.

·3·

THE DANCE OF CREATION

WHAT IS THE MEANING OF DANCE? Rhythmic
movement. What is music? Rhythm. When your life
flows in rhythm, you are creative; you are original.
So call life a dance, music, the art of living. We call it
cosmic rhythm. When you flow in rhythm you will see
that your body, mind and *prana* (vital complex) begin   *Prana*
to come into tune. You become an instrument of God,
unbound and free. When your whole being is in cosmic
rhythm, your every act becomes effortless—action-less
action, soundless sound. You come in tune with your
Lord, with Mother Nature, with Divine Mother. The
energy flowing through your being is indescribable and
inexhaustible.

Whatever is out of rhythm and tune with the Creator,
whether it is individuals, nations or systems, it will be
scrapped in course of time. This is the way nature works.
Those who are out of tune do not see God's play. The
river of immortality is flowing and they do not see it.   *Imm.*
The promise of salvation is given and they do not hear
it. In other words: they do not come in tune with God,
with the cosmos, until they surrender completely and
unconditionally, or until they are, sorry to say, brought
to their knees. Unconditional surrender is called "sweet
will"; the other is called "a blessing in disguise."

In this dance of creation the Lord and the Soul,   *Soul*
Purusha and *Prakriti*, are so intertwined that you do not

feel it is two—as if the Creator is dancing with Himself. And in this rhythmic life pattern there is joy. In any action that we do, whatever the circumstances, when we flow in tune with the Lord and His creation, the results will be fantastic. Everything may not happen the way you desire but it will certainly be fulfilling and satisfying. And then, if you are very fortunate, you will discover the whole cosmos, as far as your consciousness can travel, is all one, each aspect flowing in rhythm and tune. In creative living you do not feel afflictions or pain or a sense of separation. You do not miss anything. Everything flows as it should. You are both the doer and the witness, flowing in refreshing newness every moment. This is not emotion or imagination but spirituality, the kingdom of heaven, the golden age. The cobwebs of the brain are cleared; the nerves are purified and strengthened. Whether you gain or lose, you will be grateful. In this flowing river of life, you can take any amount of water you want. Plunge in—it has that capacity. But do not try to hold on to it. Consciousness held captive becomes unconsciousness. Life kept captive in pools of attachment and greed begins to decay. Dead habits are like stagnant water; there is no joy without movement.

Life is beautiful—that is how God created it. Man is the "supreme being," at least in our solar system, but selfishness makes us narrow and squeezed, lowly.

You can be compassionate to such a person but you cannot accept that situation. You may forgive untruth but you cannot accept it. You can forgive the sinner but you cannot accept the sin. Whether you use modern, scientific language or the most orthodox, it will be the same truth. You can respect your mother and father, your elders or your neighbors, but if they are on the untruth, you cannot accept that untruth.

Nature is clean but if we misuse or spoil it, that very nature will be unnatural. The opposite of creation is destruction. The absence of light is darkness. The absence of truth is untruth. The absence of beauty is ugliness. Ugliness and darkness are not existences in their own right. Any such opposites are created by misuse, under-use or abuse. If you worship in a superfluous, showy manner, it is irreligion. Atheism is a negation of God, not an existence. We talk about such negations only because of the dualism of language and intellect. That which is Real, which is Light, which is tangible and creative, flows in rhythm and tune with the cosmos without being a victim of illusory creation. In other words, it gives you satisfaction and fulfillment. How do we apply this in relationships? If you want to flow in tune with creation, then make God your number one relationship. You cannot serve both God and mammon.

There is a story about Shiva and Parvati, the Vedic embodiment of Heavenly Father and Divine Mother. One day Parvati told Shiva, "Lord, you are always thinking you are real and I am unreal"—Divine Mother is also called Maya. "You have been saying that you, the Spirit, are real and maya is illusory. Why is it then that you can't live without me? These are modern times and we want equal freedom. You declare me before your progeny on all the planets as Divine Mother and here you are saying I am illusion! What do you mean?" Shiva kind of scratched his head and then said, "Now Honey, since you mean business I'll tell you straight. Preaching is for those who are ignorant, not for those who know. Thou, Parvati, *knoweth*. Thou should not ask this question. It is for those who are clinging to the un-divine, to illusion, to darkness. For them I preach this distinction, this discrimination. It is for those to realize the Real from the unreal, not for those who already see the Divine everywhere. Thou, Parvati, are always in my tune, perfectly one with me. This preaching is not for you but for those who still do not see the Light."

There are two kinds of maya, but they are not two separate things. Ramakrishna called them *vidyamaya* and *avidyamaya*. *Vidya* is enlightened maya; *avidya* is ignorant maya. Normal relationships are in the domain of avidyamaya—naturally, they cannot give salvation. That is the law of nature. Any discordant note, any movement out of tune in nature is rejected. Whenever movements are disturbed in the earth atmosphere or the cosmos, nature begins to bring them back into rhythm. Human clashes, whether in battles, wars, or even two individuals fighting, are not what nature is supposed to be. Nature reacts to such disturbance by creating earthquakes, volcanic eruptions, storms and even disease. When your health, mind, body and life are out of tune, then disease begins. Ayurveda, the Vedic system of health, teaches that disharmonies in the body create dis-ease. Any mental disturbance or tension is simply being out of tune with your Spirit, your God or your Guru.

Maya is paradoxical; Truth is not paradoxical. Parvati asked Shiva, "Lord, do you think anyone can live without relationships, therefore without maya?" He said, "Look, Parvati, maya is not to be shunned if you are in tune with her. If you are in rhythm, flowing in tune with each other, that is perfectly all right. If you fight with the current of the river, you will drown. You have to swim in such a way that you and the water are enjoying each other." This is the meaning of Radha-Krishna: Oneness.

Whatever makes you noble, whatever expands your consciousness, is religion. According to your temperament, according to your free choice, you choose from traditional, liberal, modern or ancient paths, whatever makes you truthful, joyful, giving and righteous. Your True Self dictates, not your ego or selfishness, because that will degrade you. Whatever your inner voice, your Spirit and your conscience tell you, follow that. There is a saying in India: "You may be born in a church; don't die in a church." Relationships exist as very temporary phenomena. They are to be sustained but they are not eternal. You cannot put relationships above your God, your Divine, your Truth, your Light, your true identity. Everyone is busy trying to find their identity but they are trying to find it in someone else or something else. Your True Self is your Purusha, your Spirit, the Reality on which you play the rhythmic dance of maya. If you are firm in your footsteps, everything around you dances perfectly.

Your whole life has to be homogeneous, a totality. A partial view of life will never be satisfying. It is not the relationships that are wrong but that partial view of life. If you want to live consciously and awakened, if you want to live in your true nature, then avoid falsehood and any acts without merit. Let life flow around you and through you. Do not grab it. Leave your hands open. That is the way you will come in tune and begin to truly dance.

Man was made in the image of God—we should be godly. Why should there even be scope for hypocrisy, betrayal, negativity or selfishness? Man can degrade himself or can make himself divine—whichever we choose. Putting on a badge of religion does not make us religious. It is what we *are* that makes the difference. If it is Real, it is Real; if it is not real, it is not real. How can the non-real exist? The simple Vedantic reply is: the non-real does not exist. Words and thoughts are a part of perception; they say things but that does not make them real. I may show you the moon in a reflecting pool but it is not the real moon. Then how does it reflect? This is the whole phenomenon you are trying to know.

Truth radiates and we see its reflection. All the discoveries and investigations, systems and "isms," are a reflection. That reflection is so real and tangible for us that we cannot leave it. This is what sages call dead habits, ignorance or delusion. Since this is so real for us, the Truth, Light and God are as if nonexistent. Therefore we worship mammon. You cannot win over God. You cannot reject Him and have your own will. Your true identity is *true* identity. If you miss it, you miss it. Therefore I always say: do not use intellect too much. Use it to discriminate: what is the shadow and what is Real. Beyond that, intellect has no meaning.

You have put too much faith in an unreal reflection. Howsoever you may love the reflection, it is not going to be Real. See it with sage-like eyes, knowing that the Reality is something else. Just abide by that. You are not negating the reflection. Let it remain. But let your eyes be on the Reality, God, Light, the Absolute. Then you will play with the reflection very well. When you perceive in this way, you are no longer a perceiver. You are *That.* You know that the reflection is simply vibratory, and this releases you. It gives you salvation, emancipation. When you realize your Spirit, your Light, you will play very rhythmically, in tune. You will *know* how to dance.

Being in tune is not mutuality, neither fighting for equal rights nor exploitation. Exploitation can only exist as long as there is self-interest. As long as you are seeking your selfish ends, you will be vulnerable to exploitation. As long as you are greedy, you can be deceived. As long as you have attachments, others will take advantage of you. If you are in tune with your neighbor, with your work environment, with the life around you, you do not have to fight for rights or interests. Come in tune and you will have these. Therefore selfishness has no meaning; taking sides and favoritism have no meaning, and so on. When you flow in tune with creation, beautifully and sweetly, you will see the supreme purpose of life: to dance in joy and to *know.* The sages call this *satchitananda*—existence, consciousness, bliss. This is the purpose of life, to which man has to evolve. Any other purpose is fictitious and superfluous.

Whether you are old or young, your goal is to awaken. Whatever losses or gains you have, do not give them serious thought. Play your part. Flow in tune. What is gone is gone. Whatever will come will come. Keep your peace. Then only can you help others. If you are disturbed, what can you do for others? You may be blaming others but you have not thought of pointing a finger at yourself. Who are you to be claiming something from others? Therefore begin to have control of your life. God will never leave you. Flow in rhythm and joy at God's Feet. There is no other rescue. Ask yourself: have you hugged the Feet of the Lord with such joy and longing that you no longer have any questions or doubts? When He tells you the truth, are you receptive? Your life is yours but not without Him. He is your core. You cannot live your life without Him. If you are trying to do that, you are creating an exercise in futility and that is why mistakes and losses happen. Surrender unto Him; you will be perfectly in tune.

Divine Mother is so beautiful. Once you behold Her you will find that beauty everywhere. It is so satisfying and completely fulfilling. We cannot exist without God and Divine Mother. This is what we have to realize. Whatever your pattern of life, see that you flow in tune with God, your Guru or Master, and then everyone and everything around you—nature, birds, flowers, trees, and even the seeming chaos of the world—will flow in rhythm. You will feel in peace. To flow in rhythm and tune is to merge and be one with the Lord.

Come back to *sadhana*, practices, such as meditation. When you begin meditating we say: "Sit in such and such posture, look to the north or east, close your eyes, have a picture of your Master or God or a cross or Om, burn incense, fix your gaze between the eyebrows..." We give it a form. Why? You are not yet selfless. If you come to me and you are perfectly selfless, I will not give you any technique. I will just touch your head and you will be in ecstasy. The form or technique is given when you are not perfectly selfless. You begin by dancing with form but once you get free from it, because of selflessness, you are consciously creating whatever you *will*. God wills and it happens. He maintains the balance of the universe in such a perfect dance of particles and waves that it forms a cosmic ballet. To visualize this you have to go very deep in meditation, beyond techniques and forms. It is spontaneous creation, moment to moment.

Simply following techniques eventually becomes repetitive and monotonous. It does not give you joy. You may accomplish it very nicely but it is not creative. God's creation is ever-changing every split second. Think of billions and billions of years and how many patterns must have formed—innumerable—and no two the same. This is called immortality. Anything that is limited or repetitive is mortal. Immortality is ever-new, ever-fresh spontaneity. To reach there you have to be very, very selfless in *everything* you do. Then you are qualified for divine life, not otherwise. The way is through you, by you, for you to come to that freedom, that boundlessness and eternity—provided you are perfectly selfless.

True devotion is born out of selflessness. Therefore true love also. And without true devotion and love you cannot have ecstasy. Ecstasy is the climax of bliss. This is expressed through the movements of the Lord. When you are in tune with your Lord there is no misery. You realize that you and your God are one. You become the Creator. Divinity is within you. You have heard it, you have believed it, but you have never cared to *invoke* that God within you. You are so busy wanting this and that, holding on to this and that, running after this and that. The whole world is busy with this and that. God does not mind because He has no mind. He is so full; He has no need of a mind. When you come in tune with your Spirit you will also get freedom from your mind.

If you are trying to be free without invoking the Lord within, you will not succeed. There is only one key and God has kept it with Him: when everything else fails, come to Him. In between, try your luck.

Whatever you do, do it in a rhythmic and selfless way. We call it *lila*, divine play. It is God's cosmic dance and drama. Come in that tune and you will play very nicely. No one has to teach you. If I am teaching you it is only because you are not selfless yet. The day you will be selfless, I will not teach you. I will simply impart to you. When you become selfless, God makes you see the Light. You may have read the story of Sri Ramakrishna. He put Vivekananda down on the ground and got on his bosom. And that bombastic Vivekananda said, "Lord, what are you doing? You're a mad man." The whole room and the walls were revolving and Ramakrishna told him, "I'll show you the Light." And Vivekananda said, "I've got my father and mother at home." Then Ramakrishna released him, saying, "Okay, get up and go home. There are karmas yet."

When that moment comes it brings up your false security. God is so merciful, He will not laugh at you. He will simply vanish. And you lose both God and security because security is fictitious. Having our security, we are still insecure. Is there any security higher than God? Try to understand the inner value of selflessness, not just doing something for someone. That is not necessarily selflessness; it can be quite selfish. To the degree you are selfish you miss God. When you thoroughly understand the value of selflessness you are nearing God. Meditate selflessly and your mind will get purified. Love selflessly and your heart will get purified. Act selflessly and your senses will get purified. Grow into that. It will bring you to ecstasy.

Your soul wants to be free. Then only can you dance in ecstasy. If your feet are tied up, how can you dance? You have to be freed from selfishness where you exist. Whatever you are doing, thinking and feeling, be selfless. In your loving, in your sleeping, eating, walking and working, be selfless. Do not think too much. Ecstasy is not for thinkers. It is for the God-intoxicated. This madness is born out of egolessness.

What you do is important but more important is your attitude, your inner feelings. God sees that. He knows what you *mean*, not what you say but what you *are*. We may try to explain, to justify our case, but there is no need to tell God what He already knows. On the contrary, we must listen to what He tells us. In order to listen we must be silent. Be still and know. Knowledge is not born in language or thinking; it is born in silence. When your mind is still, the Light shines. Then you will see the whole cosmic dance—how it moves, creates and dissolves; how every split second it changes patterns, colors and sounds. At that moment you are freedom and bliss—*Satchidananda*.

·4·

THE ILLUSION OF SPACE, TIME AND EGO

IF ALL THE CLOCKS AND WATCHES in the world were to stop, would time still exist? Watches and clocks do not make time, nor do they regulate time. They are simply machinery measuring a rhythmic pattern of repetition upon which we impose our conception of time. In absence of clocks, the movement of heavenly bodies would not stop and actually we base our time conception on the sunrise and sunset. In Sanskrit this conception is called *prahara*, a pattern that you create. If in your concentration or meditation you focus upon one thing completely, your mind stops. Time and space cease to exist. They are only conceptions.

We impose certain things upon time: "At twelve o'clock I should eat." Actually we should eat when we are hungry; twelve o'clock is a conception. I am trying to make you understand how conceptions are illusions, and therefore time is illusion. We have solidified time by repeatedly thinking of it as being "something." We give it name and form and use machinery to calculate it, but actually time is not graspable. Even holy people will say, "It takes time to be Enlightened," but that is fallacious. The truth is that it takes no time to be Enlightened, but it takes time as far as the mind is concerned.

You have programmed your mind with ideas such as: "I'll marry, then I'll have two kids. I'll make money, we will buy furniture and have a TV in every room.

When I become rich I will retire and live off my stocks. Then I will help the poor and meditate more, pray more, and serve my Master. And then after years I will go deep into meditation." In the meantime you do not know when you will die and your whole dream will tumble down. So we say, "It takes time to Realize," since you have a lot of things to finish. As a matter of fact, as long as time and space conceptions are consciously or subconsciously occupying your mind, you will not attain Enlightenment. When you achieve perfect stillness, you Realize. But since you have other considerations, commitments, obligations, desires, plans, schedules and excuses, so many conceptions together make an illusory obstruction that will not allow you to attain Enlightenment.

You are giving importance to time, which works in the world but does not work in the Spirit. It works in the world because the world is illusion; illusion works within illusion. But as soon as you come to Source, Brahman, Spirit—when you *be still and know*—time and space stand still. Your mind stops traveling, measuring and calculating. And that is exactly the way to Realize: make your whole world stand still. If you watch waves roll upon waves, that phenomenon does not allow you to see the water clearly. To truly see the water you have to be still and unaffected, not seeing the waves. If you succeed in that, you are Enlightened. All the movements of your mind stop. You transcend time and space. The day you attain this Realization you will see that traveling to any other place in the universe does not take time. You can disappear here and reappear billions of light years away. Time is not an entity, nor is space. Both are simply illusions.

You might ask: "How does this illusion work?" If time did not exist, how could scientists calculate when a space ship will pass by Uranus or Neptune and at the right time take photographs? The answer is: within the illusion, within the dream, you can travel as much as you want, and you can calculate and measure, since it is phenomenal. Otherwise you could do the same thing without calculation or taking time. The same is true of any other force, for example gravity. As long as you believe that gravity is pulling you down, as you think so it happens. You are willing the illusory force of gravity to work as you think it should. That is a capacity of the phenomenon. But there is always transcendence beyond these laws, where you could refute the gravitational pull and magnetism. Long back I had said that there will be a time when mankind will produce spaceships that travel thousands of miles per minute, and at any given moment, they will be able to turn right or left or backward without the slightest jerk or shake. They will have overcome the gravitational force.

This is what we call "mystery," *vigyana*, or "specialized knowledge." As long as you are projecting yourself into time and space in your calculations, your measurements, your excuses, it is going to work that way. Nature is mysterious. I call her Mother. Sri Ramakrishna used to say, "Mother, have grace on me. I cannot understand all this. You tell me." This mystery can only be known within you. The things that you give power to—laws, rules, conceptions— are solidified by your giving them importance. These calculations do not give us wisdom or knowledge. We impose them upon ourselves. This whole maya or illusion works that way. It is not only a belief. Science, knowledge or wisdom work according to how you give them importance.

Today we are bound by time, but in ancient India when sages lived with their disciples in monasteries or hermitages, there was no sense of time per se. If someone asked a question about spiritual matters, the sage would not say, "At three p.m. we will meet and I will answer your question." Your mood or metabolism or biorhythms would be different at a later time. The right time to know is when you are asking the question. Time today is much more mechanized and that keeps you away from Enlightenment. Let's say you are longing for the Lord. You cannot say, "Lord, I'll practice longing for You two hours daily." The Lord may not listen, or at the most He may say, "I need twenty-four hours. Why only two hours?" You sit down at seven p.m. to long for God up to nine p.m. This is very mechanical, but we allow it because, as the English proverb says, "Something is better than nothing." At least mechanically sitting and remembering God is better than not remembering Him at all. But such conceptual living is not living. Life is living us. When you truly live you flow in tune with the cosmos. If you want to live joyfully, life should not live you. Then you are not bound by anything, yet you still do everything.

In that flowing in tune, you have a crystal clear view of the world, your family, your life, everything. Do not try to understand intellectually; just try to *see*. You will see that you love things for yourself, not for the thing in itself. You love your wife, your husband, your children, your teacher, your property, your wealth, whatever, for yourself. Yajnavalkya, who was a great Vedantic sage of ancient India, wished to renounce when nearing his old age. He had two wives, Maitreyi and Katyayani, but life had ceased to give him any fulfillment. It was like chewing gum that had lost its taste. He went to his wives and said, "I'm going to renounce, so I will divide my property between you." Katyayani was satisfied and thought that this was fair.

But Maitreyi asked, "Will all this wealth and property you leave me give me immortality?" She was a wise woman. He told her, "No, you will be as any other wealthy person would be." She replied, "Then what shall I do with it? I will go with you."

In the forest, Maitreyi asked Yajnavalkya, "Tell me more about immortality and love in the world." Yajnavalkya told her, "Look, Maitreyi, you love me for yourself." She was shocked. "How can you talk like that? I came here with you and renounced everything, and now you are telling me that I love you for my sake?" Yajnavalkya told her, "Do not get agitated. Try to see clearly. Would you have come with me if that was not what you wanted for yourself? Did you come just to be with me and to help me?" And he added, "A husband also loves his wife for himself." She was satisfied. He went on. "You also love your son for your self. It looks like you love your son for the son's sake but that is not true. You have to go very deep and see it." There is a lengthy description of this conversation in the scriptures.

Yajnavalkya told her, "You worship the sun for yourself because it gives you sunshine. You love the food for yourself. You love enjoyments for yourself. You revere your rulers for yourself, for what they give you. You respect priests and teachers for what you get from them. And as long as you are doing for the self, for ego, that ego will die and you will not attain immortality." He told her, "Try to see behind the individual soul of everyone. What is the most common factor? From where do we all come, Maitreyi?" She could see the point: if you want to be immortal, if you want to go beyond all conceptions, if you want to know your true Source you have to become completely still and transcend time and space. With purity of heart, your concentration and focus will develop to know this: there is only one Truth, one Reality.

It is hard to transcend time and space before finishing with all the other conceptions. Practically all conceptions are dependent upon the conceptions of time and space, so you cannot take away that foundation and make all other conceptions fall like a pack of cards. If you could do that, it would be easier, but it does not happen that way. Let us say you are meditating in order to Realize. You are doing this in time and space, so you meditate in order to transcend time and space. If you reach that Realization, gradually as you open your inner eyes you will see that the first creation manifesting from Spirit is shining Light. In that Realization you will be blissful. Love will spring forth automatically. You have to go very deep to experience this.

You love your daughter, your son, your husband, your teacher or your friend, but as soon as someone tramples on your ego, your love evaporates. You reply back in a hurting manner. That is why sages say that human nature is primarily selfish. If your motive is not served, out of courtesy you may outwardly let it go, but you will invariably harbor it subconsciously. Does this mean there are no selfless people on earth? Some are more selfish; some are less so. When a person is less selfish, it looks like selflessness, but if you could perceive deep within you would see that it is for the self. This is not a cause for gloominess. The world is made of these illusions of the ego, so it has to be egotistical, but the degree of egotism is more or less in each individual.

Only Enlightened Souls are truly selfless. Those rare souls who have merged with Brahman, who have seen God, are truly selfless because they are no longer individuals. As long as you are individual to any degree, you are bound to be selfish up to that degree. Maitreyi was horrified and asked Yajnavalkya, "Then is there is no hope for any human being?" He said, "There is a way out. We do not have to remain this way. You have forgotten your true Essence, your true Spirit. Get back to that. That will be divine life. Thou art *That.*"

Where is time and space in this? Let us say you are making a table. It has measurements: length, breadth and height. That means you are talking about dimensions—space. Now it may take ten hours to build it—time. But what is the table itself? It is a conception.

Before those pieces of wood took shape you imposed your conception of a table on them. The tree did not cut itself into logs and travel to your house to say: "Make me into a table." In your mind you conceived of a table, then you began to work within time and space to create it. This is conception working within time and space, conceptions rolling upon conceptions.

The worst fallacy of ego is this: that it does not take *itself* as a conception. Even when we believe that the world is illusion, we continue to believe: *I am real.* This percolates into human nature. You think, "That person is bad. I am not like him." All the time "me" is better in some way than others. The world may be illusion; wealth, property, everyone and everything else may be illusion; but I am real. We have carried on this fallacy for millions of years. Vedanta says this forgetfulness is the crux of the problem, the greatest illusion of all. The ego does not want to hear: "You are illusion." Ego wanders and wanders: to the Himalayas, to forests, caves, teachers, scriptures. After years or decades of wandering, if I ask, "Have you achieved Realization?" you will say, "No, not yet." "Why don't you do this or this?" "Oh, the world is illusion." All the time, "the world is illusion"—and "me" is not!

Vedanta says: "Ego has to *merge* in Brahman, your Source." You are the illusion from which all other illusions sprang, the very root illusion. This is where the basic fallacy remains. Therefore the word "surrender" has been used. Unless your ego surrenders completely and unconditionally unto That, fighting illusions alone has no meaning. It is you who project time and space as well as excuses, justifications and understandings. So if you want to Realize, if you want to be your True Self, if you want to come back to your sweet Home, your Father and Mother in Heaven, point the finger at yourself. That is where you started all this, and that is where you will end. Otherwise, even if you demolish two conceptions, four will spring up the next day. And what does it matter if, out of a thousand conceptions, you reduce one hundred fifty? You still have eight hundred fifty.

One of the most common examples in Vedanta is salt and water. The disciple asked the guru, "You say Brahman is everywhere, all-pervading Consciousness. How can you see that and I do not?" The guru said, "Bring a glass of water and some salt." He told the disciple to put the salt into the water and mix it. When it was dissolved the guru asked the disciple, "Where is the salt?" The disciple said, "I don't see it." The guru asked, "Because you do not see it, does that mean it is not there? Taste the water at the top. How is it?" The disciple said, "Salty." He said, "Taste the water in the middle. How is it?" He said, "Salty." "Taste the water in the bottom. How is it?" "Salty." The guru said, "Isn't it salty everywhere but you do not see it?" Then the guru explained, "The things that give you gratification— good tastes, good smells, good sights, good touch— whatever little affection and pleasure you find in the world is only a pale reflection of that Brahman within."

Any joy, happiness, love or fulfillment that you feel is because Brahman is everywhere, but you are not seeing it. Whenever we think, "This person makes me happy, this person makes me sad, this thing gave me success, this thing gave me failure," we are seeing only the surface. All this is emerging out because of That which is pervading. *That* is what has to be Realized. And all this is within you. You do not need a science laboratory; you can experiment within. It is a question of longing. You long for things you desire, don't you? This longing will also make things emerge from within. What you call nothing, the void, imperceptible, is all-pervading. It depends upon how deep you go. Spiritual practice is within time and space; longing reduces the distance and the time. People travel thousands of miles if there is sufficient longing. And if there is no longing, someone may be next door and you have not seen each other for months. When longing becomes more focused, pinpointed, when ego is merged, time and space vanish. Some sages have said, "What I was seeking was just *there*, so simple."

Go within; it is inside you. It is everywhere, but you have to find it where it is accessible to you. An example is electricity. The wire has electricity but light only shines through certain fixtures. Light is everywhere but it shines in certain souls—Prophets, Enlightened Beings, gurus and sages. That is why we go on pilgrimage: we feel higher vibrations there. We seek holy places and holy personages because we feel that is where we will see the Light. God is in everyone, everywhere, and in everything. The great saint Mirabai saw God in a bowl of poison. She accepted the bowl from those who intended to poison her, believing: "This is from my Beloved." She drank it and nothing happened to her. Nostradamus saw in his bowl the future of the world, thousands of years hence. We look into bowls daily and do not see anything. If you are able to see your God, your Light, your Brahman in your son, your wife, your husband, your wealth and position, then certainly that is God. But belief is not vision. This is the difference between theory and practice. Therefore we have reverence for holy people and pilgrimages.

Forgetfulness is the first sin. The Sanskrit word is *bismriti. Smriti* is remembrance; bismriti is forgetfulness. Because you forget your true essence, someone has to tell you. Not only is the Kingdom of God within you, it is also the nearest possible to you.

But your pain and pleasure are also within you and that is where the shoe is pinching; you have to solve that problem first. Therefore sages say to take refuge in your Source. That will gradually reduce your conceptions and take you to stillness. The Light within you is a flame that has no smoke, a windless place of silence. This is Vedantic meditation: you go on focusing on the flame within until you and the flame lose separate identities. You become one with That, which is already there.

All conceptions are just illusion. Where will they go? They will not go anywhere. They do not exist. When waves roll upon waves, where do they go? They merge back into the water. A room may be dark for a thousand years, but the moment you bring in light, where does the darkness go? It vanishes. It never existed. It was an illusion. All conceptions are illusory dreams self-imposed upon Brahman, the Reality. When you wake up in the morning, where do your dreams go? Even if you want to see the same dreams the next night, you cannot repeat them. They did not exist. Therefore the Vedas proclaim that even the Vedas are illusory. You have to close your books and go within. You have to transcend all conceptions, including taking "you" as real.

Meditate upon the Light. Purify your heart so that your mind does not waver. Slowly and gradually— *shanai, shanai* is the Sanskrit word—the distance between you and the flame will reduce. Do not blame anything else. Your separation from your true identity, God, Brahman, is the cause of all your pain. Had you not left that abode you would have no problems. How many would fling themselves like mad ones without thinking or planning or any reservation? Not me, Lord, Thou. Mirabai said, "My Lord is my all!" That is pure love, pure longing, with nothing else in between. That is why only one among millions sees Him, because of all the conceptions, barriers, blocks and hang-ups, no matter what we say or try to justify. The only legitimate question that could come up is: "If everyone did this, what will become of the world?" Actually, at that end this question does not exist. Even if everyone plunged into that Light, this question would not exist. Everyone does not do it anyway. It is only you who can do it.

This is the climax of Vedanta: *Nothing has ever happened. You already are so.* Vedanta does not say, "Thou wilt be That." It says, "Thou *art* That." It does not say, "I will be Brahman." It says, "I *am* Brahman, the Absolute." Your own thinking and calculations have been your blocks. Now you are blaming conceptions and other personalities or situations, but it is all you. It is a simple thing: you are there, where you want to reach. Just open your inner eye, your inner consciousness, and you will see that what you are trying to find is there, everywhere. You were blindfolded, simply. When your eyes are opened, when you are perfectly still, you will see. The Light is always there. Reduce the distance between you and your Light and merge into That. The pure devotee longs for God alone. Vedanta says simply, "Only He exists."

·5·

UNVEILING THE SECRETS
OF THE UNIVERSE

THEY SAY THAT IN THE UNIVERSE, stars are like grains of sand on the beaches of the world; there are so many. Even if you were to travel at the speed of light for one year and return, at the end of that year where would you be? According to Einstein, an infinite amount of time would have passed. That means if you travel in space just one year at the speed of light, you will have to say a permanent good-bye to your family. When you come back, things will be totally different. Timothy Ferris said this in his book, *Galaxies.*[6] He did not use the words detachment and renunciation. However, if you achieve the speed of light within, you *become* light.

When you become light, you transcend space and time, yet you still exist in the relative plane, dealing with whatever you want. You have conquered speed but movement is still there. You are Enlightened as well as living in relativity. This you can achieve, but you forget. Then ego tries to justify many things. What do you get when you want to justify your ego? I do not think you get anything. Even despair is a kind of luxury that you cannot afford. If you go on condemning yourself, you are not going to go up. Somewhere you have to go upward or inward. Just relax and see the Light.

Nothing will give you true satisfaction if you forget the center of your existence. And for this, we should not blame things; the blame is for each of us. How much do you remember and long for the Light within you? We weep so much for sons and daughters, wives, husbands and sweethearts. All the time we are busy forgetting the main thing: longing and remembrance of the Light. That Light is within us, God is within us. What else do we need?

Then if you still want to go to another galaxy, you can. But probably you won't need to. When you are here you want to go there; if you were there you would want to come here. When you go there you say, "We have progressed." What have you done? When there are so many suns in the universe, like grains of sand, by going from one grain to another, where is the progress? There is nothing wrong in doing those things, but you *are* the universe. You are not just blood and bones and nerves. There is Light within you, be sure, and when you are still, you will see the Light.

When we say, "Make God number one for you," that number one is within your other half too—your partner or child or father or friend. Attempt other things: money, position, talent, but keep your mind on number one. You have lost nothing and gained nothing. When you are restless you do not see it. When water is restless, it does not reflect properly. You think you have lost something. Humanly, that may be so, but truthfully, nothing belongs to you. You think things belong to you and therefore when you lose them you feel pain. If you remember the main point, the Light within you, you will see that life is continuously blissful. Forget that and try to make your life happy and pleasurable, you will always miss it. This is scientific, not just spiritual. Go within to see the Light first—you will have conquered all movements and accomplished all achievements. What magic it is!

Whatever you want to achieve, be still and know. This is a fundamental point. The ambition to achieve is itself a block in achieving results, at least spiritually. Of course, you put efforts to achieve material things, but the goal, the Light within you, does not need efforts. It is by ceasing to put efforts that you Realize. Relax, go within and see the Light. Then you conquer the speed of light. You do not have to travel one hundred eighty-six thousand miles per second. That itself is another limitation. And even at the speed of light, it is a never-ending journey. But look at the beauty: it ends perfectly when you attain complete stillness. In that ending, all knowledge is inherent.

Knowledge is not achieved by going *there* but by going within what you *are.* What is within you is not *yours*—it is everywhere. This seems to be an enigma but is a simple truth: the essence of "you" and "there" is the same. Wisdom lies in knowing the here and now. "There" is relative to "here," but when you are "there," that is "here" for you. Try to catch this. You may study the menus of ten restaurants but you will have to sit down and eat at one restaurant. At that spot it will be here and now for you. Likewise, the present moment and present spot will be the place and time in which you search within.

Unless you conquer speed, you cannot hope to reach anywhere, even other galaxies. And when and where are you going to end? We already have so much on this earth. If we have exhausted everything of this earth, we may go there to plunder, but I do not think we have exhausted everything yet. For example: scientists say that if only we knew how to convert one kilogram of matter into energy, it would give electricity to the entire United States continuously for two months—only one kilogram. How many kilograms does each of us weigh? For the convenience of calculation, let's say we each weigh fifty kilograms. That means that the energy within each of our bodies can supply electricity to the USA for a hundred months.

This is what we are talking about: how to convert our ignorance into Light. That Light is within you. The higher you go in physics or any science, the more mathematics loses its meaning. You then come to laws and principles, not calculations. Once you convert one kilogram *within you* to Light, you are totally transformed. You will be all pervading—instantly appearing and disappearing throughout the galaxies. That capacity is within you—can you believe it?

When they speak of one kilogram of matter, scientists are referring to wood or iron or steel or stone, but the human body is also matter. Therefore sages of ancient times said: *Light is within you.* You can deny it. But the more you try to evade or deny it, the more you get exposed. Truth has to be first understood, then accepted, then realized. Whether you go through faith or science, if you pursue truth honestly, you will arrive at the same conclusion: Truth is one. Not only the matter outside you but your own body is a treasure house of light. As the sun gives light and energy and life, you as one being can enlighten the whole universe. This may sound unbelievable but it is true. When you settle within and relax you will find peace. Everything that was impeding you—anxiety, restlessness, fear, insecurity or confusion—will vanish like a dream.

The secret of knowing is to be here and now. There is no greater wisdom than that. It may be hard to stay on this, but that is because your mind is on other things, not because it is hard to be one-pointed on one thing. On the contrary, the easiest and only legitimate fact is: you can only be one-pointed on one point. Because your mind is focusing on many things, it is hard to focus on one thing. So you are dangling nowhere: neither the Reality nor the phenomena. Phenomena are illusive; the Reality is tangible but by not being one-pointed on the Reality, we miss it also. This is what we call confusion. "Then what should I do to avoid my confusion?" This is one of the most often-asked questions. There is only one reply: come back to that one point, here and now: Light is within you; everything lies within you.

The Light, Consciousness, Divine, God is never boring. It is inexhaustible. That is the beauty of Oneness: in that pervadedness there is no monotony. It is always refreshing, fulfilling and ever new, because everywhere you go, that is *you*. You may feel that you are searching for ten things but actually you are not. Under the garb of those ten things, what you actually need and want is *you*. And when that *you* is all pervading, you are living spontaneously.

If you could do one thing only and keep your mind on it, everything else shall follow. If you are lost in the carnival, you have to at least start searching for the exit. It is difficult to put two feet in two boats, but if someone tells you to put both feet in one boat, what is difficult about it? That is what we are trying to do.

However, everyone is busy trying to travel in four or five boats at a time, meaning relativity: pros and cons, left and right, up and down, right and wrong, good and bad, friend and enemy. That two-legged relativity, trying to be in four or five boats at a time, is confusion confounded. And while we are busy traveling in several boats at a time, which is mathematically impossible, we are trying to meditate upon God!

Gather all your fingers and toes, arms and legs, and put them in one boat. That will give you the secret. To get one-pointed you have to relax and be still. And to relax and be still, you have to make the decision to keep your mind on one thing. It needs your will. Start deciding on the one-pointedness of your soul. Your decision is paramount: Light is within you. You are the embodiment of Light. This is a very simple, natural method. You will see that things are easy if you realize that here and now, not tomorrow or ten years hence, or when you will retire to the Himalayas, or when you will meet your Guru. These are helps, but as long as you are thinking there and then, you are keeping it pending. The day and time you will decide to be here and now, wherever you are, whatever you are, you will relax. Your nervousness, depression, disappointments, confusions and heartaches will be over, just by coming back to your Self, the center of your Being.

When all your searches end, you will find fulfillment. When all your desires end, you will be satisfied. It is not in restlessness but in settling your mind that you find everything. I am not talking about renunciation of desires. On the contrary, when you have gone to the basis of all your desires, you will find fulfillment. Remember these words. Underneath every craving, every search, you are trying to find your *Self.* Therefore go within. You will know the secret of galaxies, universes. You will be the embodiment of Light moving with full Consciousness. That heritage is within everyone.

We call it Light, Consciousness, God, the Divine. Keep your mind on That. Do not try to practice to be on That. Do not fight with your mind. Be patient. Allow time to lapse. Everything else will subside if your mind is on one point. The Light is within you. Somehow you have become unconscious of it. You began to believe, *I'm flesh and bones and other things inside.* Therefore you do not see beyond it. When you believe the apple must fall from the tree, naturally it falls down. But if you had full, unflinching faith with not one percent of doubt that the apple will go up, it will go up.

It may sound crazy but it is not scientific laws that determine the creation. The creation has its own laws to safeguard it. The way we create makes the laws.

Scientists may disagree but I stand on this. Laws do not create the creation. Change the laws; creation will change. We make justifications for the way we live, for our mundane values, but when we decide to live some other way our philosophy changes. When you believe this you will believe in the freedom of the soul. Ultimate freedom is beyond space and time conceptions and laws. We are bound by laws to the extent we have created that pattern. Change the pattern—the laws change. There is a creation where you do not have to go through doors; in the fourth dimension you could go through the walls. Which laws are absolute except on their own level?

Therefore to know the Self is the highest secret. When concentration becomes your natural behavior, you create your own laws. How? When your longing and intensity for your goal is whole-hearted, concentration is not a thing of practice; it is your nature. And that is what creates. As desire creates on the material plane, on the spiritual level your whole-hearted decision creates or makes it possible. Therefore, I would not advise you to practice concentration. I stress more upon making your whole-hearted decision, because that is your Self. If you go deep within, you will see what is fragmenting your will. You will see the ten things that are holding you, the things you have nourished and cherished. They are distracting your concentration.

Stop searching. Be still and relax. You will find the answer. That is how scientists make their discoveries, in intuitive, quiet moments. Do you think Einstein worked out the mathematics of $E=MC^2$? Even scientists today are baffled how he arrived at this formula. Einstein said he got it somewhere within him. Maybe it was intuition, maybe a dream. These very high secrets are always realized in moments of quietude and stillness. It is weakness that makes us value things that have no value. And the secret of all values, our own Self, we are missing all the time.

If you could ever, by the grace of God, see your body as a dazzling inferno of Light, you would believe it. But that does not happen without your preparation. Then you could see not only your body but all bodies as flames of Light. When you *will*, one-hundred-percent, to know the secret of your own life, you shall arrive at the highest discovery: the Light, the Divine within you. The sages, Enlightened Beings and Prophets are telling us that this is possible for everyone. They show the way because potentially everyone is Divine; everyone is Light. We are made of that Consciousness.

Make a decision whole-heartedly. Ask your heart: have you made that unconditional decision? And if you do, I am sure that all disturbances will leave you. Those who seek God, He protects. Those who follow the Truth, the Truth protects. Follow the Light. You do not have to fight against darkness or untruth. You do not have to curb your mind to remove your disturbances. Make this one unconditional decision, and see the results.

ILLUSION, REALITY AND THE NEW AGE

DO YOU CHANT AT HOME?

Yes, with recordings…

That's okay. But live singing is still different, right?

Oh, it's much, much easier. Nothing like the real thing.

And what is the "real thing"?

The pure Light within us.

So that's the one thing that we should be after. What makes us not do that?

Maya.

Maya, yes, but if you had the real thing inside you, maya should not be able to disturb you, right?

I wish it wouldn't.

So you are more attracted to maya?

Not really.

But you are holding on to it.

It's holding onto me.

To you? You are the liberated one then?

No.

Maya, for those who may not know, means illusion or illusory perception. The exact definition is: apparently real but not really so. Perceptually it exists but substantially it does not. So if both you and maya are clinging to each other—

Well, apparently I can't get free of it.

If that is your struggle, to separate from maya, I do not think you will ever succeed. Let's put it this way: you can separate two things if both are concrete, but if one is concrete and the other is an illusion, that illusion has no existence of its own. So what are you separating? If I tell you to separate yourself from your shadow, how are you going to do that? It is not a separate thing that you can pick up and keep somewhere. So if maya is illusory perception, not real, then how will you separate from it?

A shadow you can see, but it is not tangible. In other words, you perceive it with your eyes alone, so it is apparent. So it is with maya. If you are trying to separate yourself from maya, you will never succeed. It is as good as putting your shadow in storage for the time being. This is one of the extreme fallacies that many, even those who are hardcore practitioners of Vedanta, do not comprehend. "I'm trying to be separate from maya…maya is bad, devilish, satanic…maya is trapping me…maya is catching me…maya is deluding me…maya is degrading me…I don't want maya!" If you are flinging your limbs around to free yourself from maya, it will never happen. The more you fling yourself around, the more your shadow copies you. So when you are desperate, your shadow is desperate too. When you shake, your shadow shakes. And when you look at your shadow, your shadow looks at you.

SO WHAT IS THE METHOD FOR UNDERSTANDING MAYA?

I guess you have to realize, "I am the Light."
So that's the original question I asked you: why
haven't you been doing that? What is the meaning of
Realization? You do not make the Real real. It is real
already. You are simply being *conscious* of the Real.
When you are conscious, the illusion vanishes. That
is the answer. So, it is not that you and illusion are
hugging each other. You are *perceiving* illusion as
Reality. When you are conscious of the real Reality,
maya does not exist. It is not an entity or an identity
or a commodity. It does not exist. And therefore you
cannot separate from it or avoid it. The more we try
that, the more we fail. If you become conscious of the
Reality within you, God within you, maya vanishes.

The shadow, illusion and darkness are synonymous,
no doubt, but *it doesn't even vanish*. Something that
never existed cannot vanish. Why? Darkness is nothing
except the negation of light. What you negate is not an
existence, so darkness is not an existence. The absence
of light may look like darkness but it is not anything.
The same thing applies to virtues and vices. What is
hatred? We feel or think that hatred is an element or
emotion of mind. Actually it is not really so. Apply the

same principle of light and darkness and you will see that hatred is simply the absence of love. We have named it hatred, so it seems to be an emotion or feeling. When somebody hates, we can see it. Now dualistically, this is true, but if you go deeper you will see that hatred is just a negation of love. Everything in the world, in duality, is like that. The absence of any particular thing is what makes us see it as a shadow, as darkness, illusion. When you let go of hatred and your heart is filled with love again, where does the hatred go? Do you keep it on a shelf somewhere? What happens to it? You can alternately hate and love, true, but both cannot exist simultaneously. When light comes, darkness vanishes.

It needs precise concentration to catch this. Let's say you enter a dark room and put a light on. If the darkness that was there was able to squeeze into a corner where you could see it as a separate entity with the help of light, it would have an existence. But it does not exist. Not only that, it never existed in the first place. You can turn off the light again and the darkness seems to be there. Does it come from outside or anywhere? If you turn on a light here, does that make the darkness deeper in another room? It does not because it does not exist. It is not a commodity, an element, an emotion or even a state of mind; it is simply negation of light.

There is a great aphorism in the Rig Veda: "Do not

blame the darkness, bring light." Apply this to virtuous, ethical language: "Do not judge others." It is another matter that we lose the higher state of mind and come down to do the same things we have been doing, in the fair name of being human. Things in this world seem concrete, tangible and perceptible only because our minds give shapes and labels to them. We give them existence. Actually maya on its own has no power to hold you— you are holding onto maya. It is *you* who are giving the power to perceptions to make them a reality for you. Try to abuse maya, blame maya, accuse maya or love maya— the same will come back to you. It is your own power reflecting back to you. We give power to maya to have a hold on us. Wherever you go, you are taking your maya there, or we commonly say, wherever you go you take your mind with you. The mind is synonymous with maya.

Whatever power you give to your mind, your mind has that power over you. We call this *samskar* or habit. "What can I do? My mind is not in my control."—as if maya is not in your control, darkness is not in your control. Now see the fallacy of this: darkness cannot be in your control because it does not exist! There is only one solution: bring in light. Just be *conscious* of the Light within, your True Self, the *real* thing, your God within. Then your mind will have no power over you. You are trying to fight with your mind or control it. This is as good as controlling the darkness—it is futile. And because the mind is habituated to externalize through the senses, you see this illusion as real. That is where the whole fallacy lies. We want to hug the shadow! Therefore sages say that maya is insatiable. It gives the appearance of satisfying sometimes but it is insatiable—the more you hug the shadow, the more you do not get anything!

One of the attributes of maya is that it is transitory. Change the circumstance; the shadow vanishes. If the sun is directly overhead, the shadow will not exist. This is the simplest truth; anything else is complex. Maya is simply the replica of true Reality. That is why it is written: God created in His own image. We are not seeing the totality because our perceptions are limited. We are seeing only a part of God's image. The creation and the Creator are one. We see the creation and lose sight of the Creator; then we try to avoid this or that aspect of creation. That is why we suffer.

You have to absorb the darkness within the Light. That is, when you are one with the Light, darkness itself is absorbed. You are trying to fight your untrue self—that is the problem—because its existence is the holographic reflection of the Reality within you. In one or the other way, we want to remain under the sway of maya, somehow clinging to it. When Light shines, the darkness does not cling to you. As long as you remain in the darkness, whether you are wailing or enjoying, the darkness envelops you.

"But what can I do?" You are the only person who could do it. You think others will do it for you? They are busy with themselves. "But I can't do everything." You did everything already! Who else did? If you want to do it, why are you not able to? Are you one hundred percent sincere and honest to do it? "I would like to." That is not the language of a sincere person. An honest approach would be, "Yes, I'll do it." Apply the same principle. You are not dishonest; you are lacking in honesty, which we have named dishonesty. The truth is, only one exists. If the relativity consisted of both elements: negative and positive, or equal and opposite, there would be two parallel existences and God would have a problem, I tell you frankly. The seeming opposite is a shadow simply, a negation, the absence of reality.

Another example is your reflection in a mirror. It seems like you but is not you. If you understand this, you will see that all negative forces are simply the absence of positive forces. This being the case, we say, "Do not judge." That is why a Prophet could say, "There is no sinner." Vedanta says that we are not sinners; we are the children of Bliss and Light. We reflect outside us what is in our own mind. And this is the whole play of hide-and-seek, light and shade, which keeps creation possible. We are giving tangible power to that illusion so that it becomes a reality for us, and therefore we experience a clash between the Real and unreal, between Light and darkness. That is why we fear darkness.

If you knew what you have to do is simply bring Light, you would not be afraid of darkness. Try it. It is spiritual, no doubt, but psychologically it is also true. Attain peace of mind and you will find peace most everywhere, if not everywhere. In other words, when you see the Reality as it is, you do not lose your peace of mind. "Okay, so what is the remedy? What is the rescue?" The method is the same for everyone. How did you attain peace of mind? How did you begin to see things clearly, as they should be and are? *By being conscious of Reality.*

"How long shall I live in this darkness?" I am reducing this whole discussion to one line: just bring Light. Or put it another way: you will live in darkness as long as you perpetuate it. Therefore the fundamental question arises: what are you doing about it? It is one thing to blame maya for holding on to you. Just reverse it: when are you going to give up maya? When are you going to dispel your own shadow? Of course, the question can legitimately arise—how to do it? That is how the path opens, through a realized Master. Jesus said, "I am the way, the truth and the life."

We often take consolation, "Since I believe in God, I am religious, I am a good person, isn't that sufficient?" If that were sufficient, why do you have complaints, regrets and whatever? You have to *remember* that you and your Creator are inseparable; you and the Reality within are inseparable; maya and God are inseparable. You have to remember that, not only believe it. Then foolishness or ignorance will not exist. But you say: "God, help me to live as I want. I will worship You. Just give privileges to me and then You can go back to heaven. I will take care of myself." In this attitude, you are separating yourself from the One you are seeking to help you. This is the first great FOOLISHNESS—in capitals—that we perpetuate all the time. We are being blasphemous, in a way, when we worship God or try to realize the Reality in order that our best interests are served. And there we lose the way. Life doesn't go smoothly as we want. Negativities make us suffer.

To live consciously, the way is shown by your Master or Lord or Spirit within, whomever you subscribe to. Your life has to be *with* that, not by you and only for you. That way of thinking is a myth because you are inseparable from God. You cannot just worship. God has to be *with* you, integral in your life, "the way, the truth, and the life."

· 7 ·

LORD SHIVA'S DANCE

THE PHYSICISTS AND SCIENTISTS of today have described the movement of particles as a dance. What they are trying to discover is the dance of Lord Shiva.

When you dance and sing the name of God, your *kundalini*[7] begins to rise, your nervous system gets lighter, your mind gets purified, and humility is the natural outcome. This is the path of devotion—where you lose yourself in singing God's Name. For those who keep to etiquette, their path is self-inquiry, analysis and auto-reflection. There is a third path in the yoga tradition that is still higher than these: go within silently and surrender.

When you are singing and dancing in devotion, you are still going through the senses, though purified. But when you surrender you do not use your senses; you just drop into silence and awakening. None of these paths is inferior; it depends upon your temperament. You will awaken as a fully conscious being, solid as the Himalayas. Storms may come and go but the Himalayas will not move.

When you drop into Silence, you awake as shining Light. Actually you come back to your original Self. And in that Realization you will see how the creation is happening in a dancing form. Where there is no fear, no shyness—there you joyfully merge unto your Lord. We call it ancient, eternal, infinite. There is a stage when you will experience creation as a dance. In spiritual language we call it ecstasy. When ecstasy expresses, it becomes dancing. In its own pristine stage, ecstasy is non-expressive; therefore it does not seem to be dancing. But if you are in ecstasy inside, all the particles within your body-mind complex are actually dancing. That is why you feel ecstasy rising up.

Any movement is not dancing, only when it is rhythmic. When you have imbalance or non-rhythmic movements, when your mind is disturbed or restless, you lose the joy and the dancing. Again when you flow in rhythm with the Lord, you feel joy and ecstasy. When you enter the ocean of awareness you will see that all the particles of creation are dancing a cosmic dance. That is being in tune with the cosmos and surrendered unto the Lord.

What is surrender actually? You are merging into the One Who is pure ecstasy. When you are in this cosmic tune, all the movements in your body-mind complex are in joyful movement. Even if you are sitting perfectly still, the particles and atoms of the universe are coming into you and going out of you *incessantly*, maintaining the mirage of stability. Your body is changing every second, like a whirlpool in which the water is incessantly flowing in and out. If you could watch those movements, you would see that they are dancing.

The amount of imbalance you experience is proportional to your un-rhythmic movements. To put it differently: to the degree you have truth in you, you are stable; to the degree you have untruth, you are unstable. Whatever is unrhythmic is chaos. And that is where you feel misery, pain, separation, lack of love, lack of satisfaction, lack of union, and all that. You might have experienced sometimes when you have a very good meditation, a tingling begins to rise up within you. You feel light and joyful all of a sudden. Whenever you are in rhythmic flow, your body and mind are in complete harmony and balance and ego dissolves.

When Lord Shiva dances he brings balance back in the creation. They say the earth shakes when Lord Shiva dances his cosmic dance, *Tandava Nritya.* Call it mythology, symbolism or realism—it is as real as any other phenomena. When the earth shakes, some die, some howl, some grieve, some faint away, some struggle, some watch what is happening, some sleep, and some go on praying, "God, have mercy upon us."

That is what we call Shiva's dance of destruction: the earth shakes, your body shakes. The transformation power of that struggle is to create balance or rhythm, and when that happens, we regain harmony and peace. The elements that are disturbing or are bringing un-rhythmic energy are purified and transformed in that holocaust. In order for the dance of destruction to subside, they say Lord Shiva's consort, Parvati, goes on praying, "Lord, now be merciful." Lord Shiva's anger, so-called, subsides. He heaves a relieved sigh and that again creates balance.

This holocaust happens when we have not paid heed to God's loving persuasions. We call it a holocaust but it is benevolence, blessings in disguise. It brings you back to the cosmic dance, and when you dance in unison, in oneness, in ecstasy, it is heaven. That is called *Golok Dham*, the Kingdom of God, the Garden of Eden, life divine. That blissful rhythm will eradicate all disease, all miseries, and all sense of separation.

To get back to that rhythm you have to first drop into silence. Without destroying anything, your being subsides. You relax those un-rhythmic movements so that you emerge in ecstasy. That ecstasy of dance is incessantly going on in your body, mind and life. One could explain it in various ways. Cooking or painting can be done in that rhythmic dance. You can sing in rhythm and flow with it. You can even drive your car from home to office in such a way that your energy flows in a rhythmic way.

Where are you when you are not in tune with this flow? You must be in your ego trip, doing for you. When you dance with the Lord you are in rhythm with the Lord, not with your ego. So this Tandava Nritya dance is God's way to bring us back into balance, individually and globally. Somewhere we have to come to balance, either by the method of destruction or by quietly merging in tune with the Lord.

·8·

BEYOND TIME AND SPACE

THE PHYSICAL UNIVERSE occupies less than one percent of all space. This means that we are primarily conscious of only one percent of creation. There are billions of solar systems and even at the speed of light it takes billions of years to cross the universe. When are we going to finish? And ultimately we carry our mind and ego wherever we go. We will build cities in space and on other planets, and yet create the same phenomena of acquiring and possessing, selfishness and fighting.

Thousands of years before Einstein, Vedic sages revealed that there are six dimensions: three of space, three of time. The fourth dimension is of time only. In the fourth dimension you do not sleep or get hungry or thirsty or tired. You do not have attachments or obsessions. It is similar to deep sleep when you are unaware or unconcerned about your home, your family, your job, money, friends or enemies. The fourth dimension opens our consciousness to clairvoyance and clairaudience. Your third eye opens and you can see light-years away. You can disappear here and instantly reappear in another galaxy.

The fifth dimension is beyond description; no language exists there. It is a state between dreams and deep sleep. Your consciousness remains in a seed form. The sixth dimension is where your ego exists without a physical or astral world. This is a beautiful point:

normally when we talk about ego, we are talking about third-dimensional ego. But where it *really* exists is in the sixth dimension. There you come face to face with your actual ego.

If you do not want to trouble yourself with dimensions, then simply go to the cause of your being, the cause of your present existence. What is the cause? Ego. Any limited existence is the creation of the unit called "I." If you transcend this I-ness you go beyond the conceivable, beyond dimensions, to Enlightenment. When you come to Enlightenment, actually you come to space. This may surprise you: space is nothing else but light. Space throughout, limitless space, is all light. All these stars that you see shining in the night seem to be the brightest points in space, but that is fallacious.

You see the light coming from the sun and moon and stars rather than in space because you are living in a three-dimensional world. When your consciousness opens to the fourth dimension you will see that space is more dazzling than the stars. Take an example on earth. Let's say each one of us is a star and in between there is space. Between each of us there is light but we do not see it. In full Enlightenment you will see the light within each of us and outside us. When you realize the Light within you, the Kingdom of God within you, it does not end in your six-foot body. It is everywhere.

The potential to reach higher dimensions is within you. You get glimpses through dreams and other experiences, because that potential wants to open. You shut it off for reasons of practicality: your job, family, home, ashram, money, food, credit cards, insurance, bank balance. These are real to you in the third dimension, but that is not the end of creation. Therefore Jesus said: "There are many mansions in my Father's house."

In the meantime you are beset with many identifications, and that is the work of ego. Even if you travel into outer space it is ego-identification, only it is rarified. Therefore Enlightenment remains far away. Enlightenment is virgin space, where there is no identification. It is beyond stars and galaxies, beyond form or creation. If you go by scientific calculations, that virgin space is billions and billions of light-years away, what we call the unknown, the unmanifested, *avyakta* in Sanskrit. Now compare that with how we are struggling to give up ego in these three dimensions. This physical dimension is one percent of creation and another ninety-nine percent is needed to give up ego. Just imagine even touching ego where it really is, in the sixth dimension.

If you want to have fun—"Let me see what is out there"— it will require billions of light-years just to see another galaxy. And there again you are beset with ego, which means you have not known the truth. Whatever equations and formulas Einstein and other scientists have given, you will never know the secret of creation until you lose your ego, until the subjective-objective relationship is transcended. When you are observing space or whatever phenomena, you are thinking or believing that you are separate. This is a fallacy. You are trying as one phenomenon to observe all other phenomena. You will never know the secret of creation by that method.

The day you become aware that this whole creation is not outside you or separate from you, you will touch upon the unified field. One corner of the whole can only know the whole when it merges into the whole. When you merge into that unity of which you are a part, you are giving up ego. But now you are trying to know the totality while maintaining ego. We say, simply merge and find your unity. This is not spirituality versus science. On the contrary, at that point spirituality and science merge. Science will one day come to this realization: that we cannot know the Truth objectively. Whatever we observe, we are creating. There will never be a time, without exception, when we will know the secrets of the universe while maintaining a separate identity.

Shouldn't we struggle to find out? If you want
to experience, fine. But if you are truly intent upon
knowing the secrets of the universe, how this creation
all started, then there is only one answer: realize the
unity of which you are a part. That means we are
talking about egolessness. Creation is a never-ending
phenomenon. Even if we travel billions of light-years
to the end of the universe, the same question will arise:
What lies beyond? It is limitless Light everywhere—
you can hardly conceive it. The very conceptions you are
making are the barriers between you and your truth. To
break those barriers, you have to give up conceptions.
Then you and your truth will be one, indescribable,
beyond time and space. There is no language there. You
cannot know the truth. You *become* the truth that you
already are.

To know, you have to *be*. At some point even
scientists will say, "We tried everything. We reached
where we could. It gave us many experiences but the
secret of creation is still elusive." It will always remain
elusive as far as ego can perceive. You do not have to
worry about where or when the universe started. The
totality cannot be calculated within time and space.
Time and space are conceptual; therefore truth cannot
be known within time and space. The solution is not in

answering your questions. When you are one with the Truth, your very questions will not arise.

When time and space conceptions are lost, no dimension exists. It is all-pervading Light, infinite and eternal. If we build telescopes of immense measurements—let's imagine one that is a thousand light-years in diameter—we will see fantastic, unimaginable things, but even then it will never end. Our resources will end but we will not discover the source of creation. If you really are bent upon knowing the truth of the universe, you need not go anywhere. Just drop your ego.

To know the Truth, you have to go deep within to samadhi. There you transcend your ego; you transcend dimensions and come to pure space, pervading Light. That is Consciousness. That Light is indescribable. In this third dimension it looks like darkness because your limited consciousness cannot behold it. An example of this is when you sleep: your room is dark and your eyes are closed. With what light are you seeing your dreams? Even if you say it is a hallucination or imagination, you are seeing something. That is called astral light. Just try to imagine what would be that Light beyond illusion, beyond dreams.

All these millions of suns are pale before that Light of Consciousness. Therefore we preach detachment, because unless you get detached from this dimension you cannot see that Light. And you do not need an apparatus. If you know the secret of Light you can travel billions of light-years in an instant. Just imagine it and be there. Even at the speed of light, it takes four and a half years to reach the nearest star. How are you going to make it to the end of the universe? In your lifetime, what can you do?

Unless you travel *beyond* the speed of light, you cannot possibly find out all that you want to know. Now here is another aspect: if you could really travel at the speed of light, your body would disintegrate. You become energy. As you become energy, where is your body identification? Now we are talking about detachment! Enlightened ones have been telling us to be detached from body identification. Science is saying the same thing. They are not telling you to be detached; they are saying that we will achieve the speed of light where matter will be energy.

You can never know the secret of creation unless you travel instantly. Any speed will limit you. But if Light is there, billions of light-years away, and that same Light is also here, why go there? Since centuries we have been thinking that space is there and Earth is here. But now we know that we are already in space—where else could we be? This fallacy occurs because we are identified here. As soon as we are not identified here, we will see it is here too. If you were living light-years away on some other planet, you would like to reach this Earth. When we are here, *that* unknown is desirable. This is what we call, in polite language, ignorance, because that which you want to know is with you already. Why don't you search there first? That Light is everywhere. If you cannot know it here, you will not know it there either.

If our purpose is to know the secret of creation, whether the Big Bang happened or not, then there is a way. You can know that here and now. We are made of that same Light. You cannot know that Light objectively. You have to merge into it. And the most amazing part is that when you know everything, you will see that nothing has ever happened. There is no speed. There is no traveling. Just as in the fourth dimension the other three dimensions are absorbed, in the fifth dimension four dimensions are absorbed, in the sixth dimension five dimensions are absorbed, and in transcendence, no dimensions exist. And where no dimensions exist, no creation exists. Therefore nothing has ever happened. In this third dimension, if I say nothing has ever been created, you will think I am foolish; there is no way I could prove it. Realized Souls and Prophets are often considered crazy because they are talking beyond dimensions. Things are practical to you on three dimensions, and they are talking from beyond dimensions, where those are not practical. When you reach that higher stage, you will understand.

This earth is moving at tremendous speed around itself and around the sun. We forget that we are actually sitting on a spaceship, only this spaceship is big, therefore we think it is static. "My home is number sixty-seven on Third Street. My office is there." We get identified. But if you could see through the window of this spaceship, I assure you that you would never get attached. Do you get attached to an airplane when you fly? You don't, because you are seeing out its window. Earth is moving around itself and around the sun, and the whole solar system is moving around itself and around something else. Whole galaxies are moving, spirals within spirals. Any conception is a barrier between you and your Truth. If you want to know the Truth, go beyond ego and conception.

You cannot see God or the Light with these eyes. Vedic sages have called it *anir vachaniya*—indescribable. But then, paradoxically, God or the Light is so *knowable* if you just go within. When the Prophets and sages preached detachment, they did very well. But you disbelieved, so God sent science to make you believe. In universities, schools and colleges, students are studying the secrets of the universe. Though they are learning academically, it is the same thing. Physicists and astronomers are trying to know the secrets of the universe. An astronaut goes into space without belongings and attachments, whether his wife or children weep or not. If someone tells him, "Sir, your country has changed, generations have passed, five hundred centuries have gone by," he will say, "Is that so?" You cannot go there without renouncing this world, which is what the sages have been saying. I am not telling you to renounce; I am simply saying to give up untrue identifications.

Ego is a barrier between you and your Truth. Conceptions are fictitious curtains. You do not need speed to know the Truth, even light speed. You get into energy and Consciousness. It is easy to know the creation once you are egoless—*very* easy. You will not have to tax your brain. Surrender your ego unto your Self, unto your God, and you will know the whole truth, here and now, wherever you are. There is no greater science than this. Some centuries back, people were executed for saying that the Earth rotates around the sun. The Earth was believed to be the center of the universe. Sages call this egoistic. Every person thinks, "I am important." It is the same phenomenon. There is no center of the universe. Five hundred years from now humanity will see the truth of it. Once you have made a center you are making a circumference, and you are creating a limit to the universe, which is absurd. Where is the center? You and I are centers. Wherever you are is a center. Between you and me it is all-pervading Consciousness and Light. Where is the center of that Light?

When we say that man is the highest species created by God Almighty, humble sages say that is ego speaking. You do not know the universe, whether there are other beings or creations. Why are you assuming we are the highest creation? And if we are God's highest creation, why are we miserable, diseased, lamenting, complaining and mortal? If we are made in God's image, then He is also miserable. With all of our poverty, diseases, wars, battles, failures, disappointments, depressions, nervous breakdowns, wanting and not having—all of this cannot be the best creation. Where is that eternal bliss and peace? Where is that immortality we talk about? That must be the center. The truth is: there is no center because there is no limit. Infinity and eternity have no center. It is everywhere—pervading Consciousness.

Any conception has to have ego existent. And if ego is existent, you cannot know the truth. God is within you. Your Allah, your Christ, your Buddha, your Krishna is within you. If you know yourself, you know everything. But you cannot know yourself while retaining ego. Ego is actually the basis for whatever miseries we experience. Sages have very clearly said, "Ego is the cause of all problems." Trying to solve problems without giving up ego is an exercise in futility.

Know yourself and you will know everything. You do not need telescopes for that. Your third eye will open and that is your telescope. God has given us this instrument with which we can see through the universe and beyond—instantly. You can see, feel, hear, touch and smell through the third eye. I am not against science; I am simply saying that the same things can be known more easily and quickly by knowing yourself. Jesus said: "The Kingdom of God is within you." Socrates said, "Know thyself." In the Upanishads the sages revealed: "Brahman is within you."

In the ultimate analysis, truth is beyond your ideas, conceptions and words. It is indescribable. You *are that* already. You have to realize what you are, not what you will be. What you will be cannot be realized. That is changing. It is tied up with time conception. Truth cannot be known within conceptualization, whether it is scientific conceptualization or religious conceptualization. Whether it is scientific dogma or religious dogma, both are barriers. Science can be as dogmatic as religion. To know the Truth, you have to go beyond all these conceptions.

It is easy, but if you are going elsewhere to *know*, you are delaying. If you say, "Let me think about it, experience it, then I'll meditate," you are putting it off, as you have put it off for so many decades or births. That which is always with you, there is nothing else to do except realize. To realize is to give up ego, whether it is a Jewish ego or Hindu ego or Christian ego or Muslim ego; whether it is an American ego, Indian ego, African ego or European ego; whether it is a male ego or female ego; whether it is a white ego, black ego, or any color ego. Whether it is a scientific ego, a religious ego or a swami ego, you have to go beyond what you are to get into Consciousness, into Light. It is you who have to realize that God is there. He has never left you.

What is the real address of God? Go on asking all over the galaxies. Then when you get very fatigued and go somewhere to rest and relax, you will find peace. Somebody tells you, "Unless you become a Hindu or Christian or Buddhist you cannot realize God." Okay, then you change your religion. Go on changing your religion, God is never there. You have to forget even where you are, what you are—any identification, whether it is religious, scientific, national, political or economic.

This is where you go beyond "isms" and dogmas, when you are not bound by any habitual conception.

Light shines everywhere, within and around you. Whether you are a sinner or a virtuous person; forget these conceptions. What you have done is done. You have to realize what you *are*. Go into that transcendence; you will see that it absorbs everything. It is all Light. Nothing has ever happened. An atom shines here, here, here in such a consecutive manner that it forms a succession that you call speed. It is not really so. Speed is an illusion. An example of this is a motion picture. People and images seem to be moving but it is an illusion. The entire universe is the same. From atom to atom it happens in such an accelerated way that to your gaze it looks like motion, but it is not. A time will come when scientists will tell you that nothing is traveling.

When we preach about detachment, non-possessiveness, non-greediness, it is only to release your consciousness from the bondage and clinging with which you are identified. When you release your consciousness, you are Liberated. Then if you want to go there and know, instantly you can vanish here and reappear there. The very next moment you could be billions of light-years away. You transcend speed and motion. Nothing else will give you satisfaction and bliss. We have tried everything. Any station in life, any possessions or relationships—do they satisfy us fully? Whether through science or spirituality, you can never be fully satisfied with untrue identifications. The simplest truth is: *Know thyself.*

IN RADIANT EXPANSE OF LIMITLESS SPACE

by Swami Amar Jyoti

In radiant expanse of limitless space
where no path is fixed
you can fly wherever you want, free
if you can renounce the burden
of hope and despair
the temptation of
degrading attractions

Open the wing of dispassion
and the wing of devotion to the Supreme
and with the arrow's swiftness
they will carry you into that realm
where there is no bondage of any kind
no darkness, no death
only Light

NOTES

1 Brahman

In Vedic wisdom, Brahman is the unchanging, infinite, immanent, Supreme Reality.

2 Samadhi

Spiritual absorption or oneness realized through deep meditation.

3 Vedanta

Vedanta is one of the world's oldest religious philosophies. It affirms the Oneness of God or Pure Consciousness pervading all existence and the divinity of the soul. Based upon the Vedas, the most ancient scriptures known to man, Vedanta means literally, "the end of all knowledge." Vedanta is the nondualist search for God or Self Knowledge.

4 Shankaracharya

Adi Shankaracharya, one of the most brilliant minds of ancient India, was a great sage and philosopher. He lived for only thirty-two years (788-820 a.d.) but his achievements were unparalleled. He propounded the Vedantic tenet that Brahman the Supreme and man are of one Essence and that all people should strive to realize this Oneness.

5 Aham Brahman Asmi

Aham Brahman Asmi: "I am Brahman" (Brhadaranyaka Upanishad 1.4.10 of the Yajur Veda)

6 Galaxies

Sierra Club Books, 1980

7 Kundalini

Through various practices, including purifications, *pranayam, mantra* and meditation, the initiated adept gradually raises the "serpent power" of the kundalini from the base *chakra* upward until it reaches the crown chakra, the *sahasrara* "thousand-petalled lotus," resulting in full Enlightenment.

BIBLIOGRAPHY

All Satsangs listed below refer to live recordings (spiritual discourses) given by Swami Amar Jyoti.

CHAPTER ONE
Unlocking the Mysteries of Creation
Edited from the Satsang: *The Dream and the Dreamer* (R-5), given in 1976 at Sacred Mountain Ashram, Boulder, Colorado.

CHAPTER TWO
What is Illusion? What is Reality?
Edited from the Satsang: *The Light Within Illusion* (K-135), given in 1991 at Sacred Mountain Ashram, Boulder, Colorado.

CHAPTER THREE
The Dance of Creation
Edited from the Satsangs: *The Dance of Life* (A-32), given in 1986 at Sacred Mountain Ashram, Boulder, Colorado, and *Dance of the Universe* (R-11), given in 1978 in San Bernadino, California.

CHAPTER FOUR
The Illusion of Space, Time and Ego

Edited from the Satsang: *The Illusion of Space, Time and Ego* (R-84), given in 1986 at Sacred Mountain Ashram, Boulder, Colorado.

CHAPTER FIVE
Unveiling the Secrets of the Universe
Edited from the Satsang: *Mass, Energy and Light* (O-18), given in 1980 at Desert Ashram, Tucson, Arizona.

CHAPTER SIX
Illusion, Reality and the New Age
Edited from the Satsang: *Illusion, Reality and the New Age* (R-103), given in 1990 at Countryside Ashram, Rockford, Michigan.

CHAPTER SEVEN
Lord Shiva's Dance
Edited from the Satsang: *Lord Shiva's Dance* (O-19), given in 1982 at Glacier View Ranch, Ward, Colorado.

CHAPTER EIGHT
Beyond Time and Space
Edited from the Satsang: *Beyond Time and Space* (O-17), given in 1979 at Desert Ashram, Tucson, Arizona.

ABOUT THE AUTHOR

SWAMI AMAR JYOTI was born on May 6, 1928 in a small
town in northwestern India, not far from the banks of
the Indus River. Much beloved by family and teachers,
He shocked everyone with the decision to leave home
a few months before college graduation, saying, "I
would like to read an open book of the world for my

education." At the age of nineteen, without money or any particular destination, He took the first train He found, eventually arriving in Calcutta. It was 1948 and thousands of refugees from East Bengal (now Bangladesh) were pouring into West Bengal each day. Living on a railway platform near the border of India and Bangladesh, He soon headed the entire volunteer corps there, working tirelessly twenty hours or more each day. After about ten months, the flood of refugees subsided and He returned to Calcutta. There a government officer who had witnessed His work at the border offered Him a high government position for rehabilitation of refugees, but He turned it down.

He lived in Calcutta and later on the outskirts of the city in a quiet ashram. It was during this time that visions began awakening in Him. He began to meditate and do yoga and attended *puja* (traditional worship) at a nearby temple of a well-known saint. In a short while He "knew" His life work. As He described it, He picked up there from where He had left off in the last birth. Very soon He traveled to Himalaya where He lived in silence and meditation for about ten years, one-pointed on the goal of Liberation. Many places of pilgrimage were visited during those years, walking on foot many miles each day. But a small cave at Gangotri, the temple village near the source of the Ganga River, was the place of His greatest spiritual disciplines, awakenings and, finally, Illumination.

In 1958 He took *Vidyut* (lit. "lightning") *Sannyas*, a form of monasticism that is Self-initiated, at the holy site of Badrinath of Himalaya, taking the name Swami Amar Jyoti (Swami—Knower of the Self; Amar Jyoti—Immortal Light). Later He descended into the plains of India for His God-given mission to the world. The first ashram Gurudeva founded was Jyoti Ashram, under Ananda Niketan Trust, located in Pune, Maharashtra, India. Throughout the years after leaving home, His mother had never ceased searching for Him and awaiting His return. In answer to her prayers, He settled in Pune where she could be near Him.

In 1961 Gurudeva accepted an offer by a devotee to visit the United States. Again He traveled unknown, though soon attracting many who had never seen such a holy man. Eventually He was persuaded by the sincerity of American disciples to establish Sacred Mountain Ashram in 1974, followed in 1975 by Desert Ashram. Both ashrams are a part of Truth Consciousness, a nonprofit organization that serves as a vehicle for Gurudeva's work in the United States.

The spiritual awakening on earth that Gurudeva reveals is the glorious destiny of mankind, once freed from our limited identity of self. Lovingly and ceaselessly He continues to uplift and purify each of us for this awakening, for His way is the ancient relationship of the Guru to the disciple, the candle lit directly from the burning flame of Truth. He constantly reminds us that we are at a breakthrough into a new age where religions will be transformed into direct awakening and communion with our Highest Source. Like a mother whose love knows no bounds for her child, the Guru guides and nurtures the disciple on his or her own path to Perfection, revealing in Himself the attainable Reality of God Consciousness.

After four decades of continually traveling in the United States and abroad, giving Satsang and Retreats, establishing ashrams and guiding innumerable souls to higher consciousness, Gurudeva took *Mahasamadhi*— conscious release of the mortal body—on June 13, 2001 in Louisville, Colorado. According to His wishes His *Asti Kalash* (urn containing Sacred Remains) was brought back to Jyoti Ashram by disciples from India. Within a year a *Samadhi Sthal* in the form of a pure white marble pyramid was created for permanent consecration. Two years later, in May 2005, His white marble life-size *Murti* (sacred image) was dedicated in this same Samadhi Sthal. Gurudeva's recorded Satsangs and books, as well as "A Biography in His Own Words," *Immortal Light: The Blissful Life and Wisdom of Swami Amar Jyoti*, are available at *TruthConsciousness.org*.

TRUTH CONSCIOUSNESS AND ASHRAMS FOUNDED BY SWAMI AMAR JYOTI

FOUNDED IN 1974 by Swami Amar Jyoti, Truth
Consciousness is a nonprofit spiritual organization
that maintains ashrams based upon *Sanatana
Dharma* (the eternal religion) and devoted to the
unfolding of consciousness. They are universal and
nondenominational, respecting all Prophets and faiths.
The ashrams offer programs year-round and all sincere
seekers are welcome. Satsang is held weekly on Sunday
and Thursday, preceded by chanting and Aarati followed
by meditation. Sadhana (spiritual practices) and karma
yoga (selfless service) are an integral part of life for
both ashramites and laypersons who wish to imbibe
Gurudeva's teachings and blessings. The books and
recorded Satsangs of Swami Amar Jyoti on CD/MP3,
Light of Consciousness—Journal of Spiritual Awakening,
and other publications by Truth Consciousness are
available at online bookstores, and at the ashrams below.

Sacred Mountain Ashram

10668 Gold Hill Road, Boulder, CO 80302-9716

Ph: 303-447-1637

Desert Ashram

3403 West Sweetwater Drive, Tucson, AZ 85745-9301

Ph: 520-743-0384, Publications: 520-743-8821

In India under Ananda Niketan Trust:

Jyoti Ashram

68 Lulla Nagar, Pune 411 040 (Maharashtra), India

Ph: 91 202 6832632

36⟩ Joy

God)

3- has **3** parts
  1. Creator ———— Brahma
  2. Preserver ———— Vishnu
  3. Transformer ___ Shiva

(10) Our World of GOD —(11) THREES
                          TRINITY
13 Creator is Essence—
           SPIRIT + Light

Creatrix
She
22

God
7- Within you
8 only One

CREATION
4- I (ego) = 1st Creation
   └ has limited Will

12- FORM + Name
13 is change
26 SAME

Will
4- God wills
   Man desires

Matter
20

Nature
37

| Consciousness |
4) Basis of = (Desire)
       of EGO

5= Motion ← creates
    =   Vibe (Wave)
Beginning
  of Dream

11) Conc. (Light) awareness = GOD

14 - Unlimited = Bliss
19) Conc. is Light ? = 20)
   36)

| Super Conc.)
   6 - 7 Samadhi

| Reality | is one continuity
12/ 19

| Maya or
| Illusion |
20-21 ❀
22

| MIND |
21/24 - 25/28

| LIGHT |
XII
14 (awareness)
19..20
21 (Matter) 22
25 | 29 ~ Illusion -30
37

| SPACE |
12

| Enlightened |
XIII Sage
AWAKE = 5

| Cosmos |
23 | 36

| The Dreamer |
3 | 5 is he
5 AWAKE
6 AWARE
7 = ONE

| DREAMS |
5
4 jumbled Vibes (of Mind)
11 — All is ~ Dream
 └ DRAMA
13

| EGO |
105 | 4
5 - Holds it all
     Together
24